The Successful TA

The **On Campus** imprint of UBC Press features publications
designed for the diverse members of the university community –
students, faculty, instructors, and administrators. **On Campus** offers a
range of interesting, sometimes unconventional, but always useful
information. All **On Campus** works are assessed by experts in the
field prior to publication. To ensure **On Campus** materials are easily
obtainable, they're made available for free download in
digital format or for purchase in print.

Resources for students are designed to help them successfully
meet the intellectual and social challenges encountered at university
or college today. The inaugural book in the **On Campus** imprint was
the highly successful *How to Succeed at University (and Get a Great
Job!): Mastering the Critical Skills You Need for School, Work, and
Life*, which is also available in French from University of Ottawa Press.
Subsequent books have been *It's All Good (Unless It's Not):
Mental Health Tips and Self-Care Strategies for Your Undergrad Years*,
by Nicole Malette, and *You @ the U: A Guided Tour through
Your First Year of University*, by Janet Miller.

To find out more about **On Campus** books,
visit www.ubcpress.ca or follow us on social media.

THE SUCCESSFUL TA

A PRACTICAL APPROACH TO EFFECTIVE TEACHING

KATHY M. NOMME **AND** CAROL POLLOCK

31 30 29 28 27 26 25 24 23 22   5 4 3 2 1

Printed in Canada on FSC-certified ancient-forest-free paper (100% postconsumer recycled) that is processed chlorine- and acid-free.

Library and Archives Canada Cataloguing in Publication
Title: The successful TA : a practical approach to effective teaching /
Kathy M. Nomme and Carol Pollock.
Other titles: Successful teaching assistant
Names: Nomme, Kathy Margaret, author. | Pollock, Carol, author.
Description: Includes bibliographical references.
Identifiers: Canadiana (print) 20220131694 | Canadiana (ebook) 20220131708 |
ISBN 9780774839082 (softcover) | ISBN 9780774839099 (PDF) |
ISBN 9780774839105 (EPUB)
Subjects: LCSH: Graduate teaching assistants. | LCSH: College teaching –
Handbooks, manuals, etc. | LCGFT: Handbooks and manuals.
Classification: LCC LB2335.4 .N66 2022 | DDC 378.1/25—dc23

UBC Press gratefully acknowledges the financial support for
our publishing program of the Government of Canada (through
the Canada Book Fund), the Canada Council for the Arts,
and the British Columbia Arts Council.

Printed and bound in Canada
Set in Ingeborg and BentonSans by Gerilee McBride
Copy editor: Lesley Erickson
Proofreader: Carmen Tiampo
Cover designer: Gerilee McBride

UBC Press
The University of British Columbia
2029 West Mall
Vancouver, BC V6T 1Z2
www.ubcpress.ca

To our families, for their love and support

CONTENTS

THE SUCCESSFUL TA

GETTING STARTED

Congratulations! You're about to assist in the teaching of a course. This is an opportunity to interact with students and influence their undergraduate education. As a teaching assistant (TA), your interactions with students, the effectiveness of the lessons you provide, and the positive support you give students can have a profound influence on classroom culture, student motivation, and the quality of the learning experience of your students. This is especially true when classes are large and if you, the TA, are the main contact with the course instructional team. So how do you get started? How do you prepare yourself for your role as a TA?

The preparation of TAs needs to be a top priority when they are part of a teaching team in postsecondary institutions, regardless of whether at universities (research and teaching) or colleges (primarily teaching). Fortunately, the importance of TA training is being recognized, and there's a growing number of TA-training programs to support novice educators in postsecondary institutions, especially in Canada and the United States. These training programs take a variety of forms; just as different institutions may promote different instructional strategies, different disciplines will also have different forms of instruction. For example, the hands-on learning experiences in the sciences, engineering, home economics, pharmacy, and art studios will be somewhat different from seminars and tutorials in philosophy, classical studies, linguistics, and other courses in the social sciences. However, TAs are sometimes assigned to teach with little or no preparation, so we developed this guide to support TAs in their preparation for teaching.

At the University of British Columbia, we were involved in the development of the Biology Teaching Assistant Professional Development Program (known as BioTAP). In it, we combined our extensive experience in TA training with best practices published in the pedagogical literature and information available from universities across North America. Although the program is intended for TAs in the sciences, the advice we offer applies to all disciplines, whether you're involved in instructing in labs or studios, facilitating seminars or tutorials, supporting lectures in large classes, or preparing and presenting lectures. Our approach is to give you basic suggestions that have proven effective for the many TAs we've worked with over the years. We've found that best practices in teaching are applicable universally. One TA offered this comment in an anonymous survey, "These training workshops have helped me understand what's expected of me as a TA and better prepare for interacting with students." Indeed, TAs who participated in BioTAP training workshops have contributed to the advice presented here.

This guide is designed to provide you – regardless of whether you're an undergraduate, graduate student, or postdoctoral fellow new to teaching or an instructor new to supervising TAs – with practical advice on being a TA. We cover the essentials, including describing what your role could be, preparing for your first class, designing lessons and learning activities, creating an inclusive learning atmosphere, facilitating classroom discussion, teaching with technology, assessing student learning, and reflecting on your teaching. We also offer insights on best practices in teaching. If you're supervising TAs, we identify issues that new TAs may encounter and offer advice on how you can best support them.

In several chapters, we provide checklists as a quick reference for the main issues or steps to consider in preparation for and during teaching. These checklists are not exhaustive, and some items may not apply to all roles. They should be treated as a guide for making checklists applicable to your own role.

This guide doesn't address topics in depth or discuss the educational theories that support our suggestions. For those interested in a more in-depth treatment of certain topics, see "Further Resources" at the end of this book.

In addition, throughout the guide you'll find numbered scenarios describing situations we've encountered or TAs have described to us. We challenge you to devise your own responses to the situations presented. At the end of each chapter, in "Possible Scenario Responses," we provide some suggestions for how you could effectively address these types of situations. And, if you're asked to assist in TA-training sessions or preparing and offering workshops, we provide some suggestions in the Appendix, "Developing Training Opportunities for TAs."

Teaching is exciting and rewarding, and we hope you'll find the information here useful. TA-training programs are often constrained by the time allocated to sessions. They can't address all aspects of teaching. We hope this guide will be a valuable supplement to other training you may receive. At first, you may encounter challenges, but there are many rewards to be gained from interacting with students and facilitating their learning. Be assured that confidence, effectiveness, and expertise in teaching often come with experience in the classroom and familiarizing yourself with educational theories and the literature on the practice of teaching (pedagogy).

We hope the information in this guide will help you get started in your preparation so you can approach your teaching with confidence, be a more effective teacher, and, most importantly, enjoy the experience!

STEPPING INTO YOUR ROLE

You've just been assigned to your first TA position. What's involved? The primary role of a TA is to support the course instructor or coordinator in facilitating student learning. Your role and level of involvement with students will vary depending on the needs of the instructor, the course design, and the number of students in the course (whether it's a single, relatively small-enrolment course or a large multisection course).

These are some of the different possibilities:

- **Large classes:** you may be asked to facilitate activities by interacting with students, answering questions, and assisting with classroom duties, and you may even have the opportunity to give a lecture or two.

◇ **Small-group meetings such as tutorials or seminars:** you may prepare lessons and facilitate discussions and activities.

◇ **Laboratory or studio courses, field trips, or other practical components:** you may present introductory instructions or demonstrations, supervise, and interact with students.

◇ **Online courses:** you may not interact face-to-face with students but may be expected to communicate electronically to provide direction and answer students' questions.

◇ **Grading:** you may assess student learning by marking assignments, presentations, quizzes, and exams. If you're primarily a marking TA, you might interact indirectly with students, assessing their work by following instructions from the instructor.

◇ **Primary instructor:** you may be responsible for all aspects of teaching a course, including preparing and facilitating lessons and activities and designing and marking assessments. If this is the case, Chapter 3 can help you get started.

Whatever your role or combination of roles, you'll be supporting student learning and making an important contribution to the teaching team.

MEETING WITH THE INSTRUCTOR OR COURSE COORDINATOR

Arrange to meet with the instructor or coordinator at the beginning of the term or semester, preferably before the course starts and when your TA contract begins. During this meeting, discuss your role, identify responsibilities, and clarify expectations for teaching times and the hours per week required outside of scheduled teaching. Ask about the structure and size of the course and where, when, and for how long the classes meet. Ask if the course format is lecture only, or if it has seminars or tutorials. Alternatively, the course may have hands-on components such as labs, studios, or fieldwork. Clarify your involvement. If you're required to attend lectures, ask whether you'll be interacting with students and helping with logistics and activities.

If you're unfamiliar with the course, find out or ask about its goals and the academic level of the content. Are there assignment due dates? Are there resources such as a syllabus, texts, manuals, or readings that you'll be required to be familiar with? Many courses have an online component, so be sure to request access to the course management system and other electronic resources. Consider your comfort level with the content. If you have little background in some aspects of the course, you may need to put more effort into preparing for your role. If, however, you have sufficient expertise in the subject, ask if there's an opportunity to present a lesson or a full lecture; if you do, ask your instructor or coordinator to provide a teaching evaluation, which you can use for job applications. Preparing and presenting lectures is excellent practice for future employment, whether in academia or elsewhere. In many disciplines, you may be asked to give a seminar, lecture, or presentation as part of the job interview.

Most TAs interact with students in smaller tutorials, seminars, or labs. Ask how the sessions are conducted and whether the lessons for these sessions will be provided or whether you'll need to select or even create relevant resources. Determine if you need to prepare and make copies of teaching materials, including discussion questions, quizzes, and other assessments. If you're teaching in a lab or studio, ask if you need to set up materials, do demonstrations, and be involved in the cleanup after each session. If the course has a field or community-outreach component, ask if you'll be involved in making the necessary arrangements.

In your discussion with the course instructor or supervisor, also ask how you'll be expected to support and communicate with students (if at all). Courses may have a policy on the means of communication, such as through electronic bulletin boards, course management systems, or other messaging tools. If you'll be answering student questions through email, ask if you must use a platform provided by your institution and ask about the expected response time. You'll also need to know if you'll be required to hold office hours on campus or virtually. Ask if you'll be required to conduct review sessions for students and what level of assistance is appropriate as they prepare assignments or for exams. At times, students may need help beyond your level of expertise; the course instructor should provide a list of campus resources to help students either with their academic issues or personal matters.

If one of your roles is to mark assignments, quizzes, and exams, ask if you'll be provided with the questions, solutions, rubrics, and marking guides. Determine if you'll be expected to assign and record student grades, what format of record keeping is required and the procedure for submitting marks for review. In multisection courses, there may be a mechanism to ensure consistency of marking in which you'll need to participate. Find out what the course guidelines are regarding late assignments and student academic misconduct. Many courses have policies regarding the review of marked assignments or exams. Ask if you'll be expected to participate in the invigilation and marking of a final exam or project. If so, don't make travel plans until you know the exam date or when the marking needs to be completed.

Once you've determined your role in the course, review your schedule with the instructor, taking into consideration periods in the term where more time will be required. Your work hours will likely vary from week to week; however, you should be given an estimate of the average number of hours you'll be contributing as a TA. Also, note the maximum hours per week or term allowed by your institution's regulations. TA working conditions and pay rates may be determined by a union agreement. Find out if this is the case. One aspect of union agreements is the number of hours of work per week or term. This number may differ if you have a scholarship. Your hours of work should also include time spent meeting with the instructor or teaching team. These meetings may be scheduled on a regular basis or as needed.

Throughout this guide, we provide scenarios that describe situations that may arise during your experience as a TA. Consider the advice we provide and think about how you would respond. There are many ways to respond to these scenarios; the most appropriate response depends on the specific context of the course, the classroom climate, the individual personalities of the students involved, and institutional constraints. The responses offered at the end of each chapter are only a sample of possible ways to deal with a situation.

Scenario 1.1 You've just been notified that you've been assigned to a TA position that starts next week. Of the many questions you have, which five are the most urgent that you should act on right away?

ONGOING INTERACTIONS WITH COURSE INSTRUCTORS OR COORDINATORS

A good relationship with the course instructor or coordinator is key to having a positive TA experience. They are instrumental in helping prepare you for class, clarifying expectations, and explaining details regarding your role.

Course instructors or coordinators will typically provide you with guidance weekly or as needed. Throughout the term, pay attention to the hours you're spending each week on your duties. If you're spending more time than allocated, be sure to discuss this with your course coordinator right away. They can help identify ways to adjust your workload or increase efficiency and reduce time spent on certain tasks.

Your course instructor or coordinator can be consulted if student issues develop. You may have students that display inappropriate behaviour or come to you with personal concerns. Your coordinator can offer advice on how to approach these situations, provide you with resources to pass on to students, or intercede on your behalf with the students.

In addition to the course instructor or coordinator, ask former TAs in the course for insights on what to expect. If you need further clarification about the role of TAs in the program or department, there should be a unit administrator or faculty member who can review policies regarding the role of TAs. Knowing what's expected will help you focus on your contributions to student learning.

If, for any reason, you're uncomfortable approaching your course instructor, there are others with whom you can discuss your teaching-related issues. For example, you can talk to an experienced TA in the course, or the person organizing your TA training, or even the faculty responsible for TA positions. If you feel your rights as an employee are not being respected, you can verify your contractual obligations with unit administrators or consult with a TA union representative.

Scenario 1.2 As part of your hours of work, you're expected to set up before each lab and clean up after. You have a class right after the lab ends and must rush off without cleaning up. Your supervisor mentions that you're not doing an adequate job of cleanup. What should you do?

BEING PROFESSIONAL IN YOUR POSITION

As a TA, you have a responsibility to complete your assigned tasks with integrity and behave professionally toward students and supervisory faculty or instructors. Regard your TA position as you would any other paid work. Regardless of your role, you need to ensure that you're well informed on the topics and concepts, professional in your interactions, objective in your assessments, and model appropriate learning behaviours for your discipline. However, this experience is more than a job; it's also a unique opportunity for you to develop your skills as a teacher and communicator.

Plan and prepare for the tasks for which you're responsible. Students will take their cue from you as you model appropriate behaviour and language. For example, be on time for classes and meetings with students, other TAs, and supervisors. If you must be late, need to miss a meeting, or are ill and must miss a class, let your supervisor know as soon as possible. When teaching, be sure to dress appropriately for the norm of your discipline, for example, if you're teaching in a lab, studio, or professional school, there may be specific clothing requirements. Make sure AV materials are ready to use without glitches and that demonstration materials have been prepared.

Treat all students, faculty, and staff fairly and with respect and expect to be treated respectfully in return. Be professional in your interactions with students and create a welcoming, inclusive atmosphere. (See Chapter 4 for more discussion on this topic.) Because you may be interacting with a diversity of students, faculty, and staff, you'll want to take part in workshops offered by your institution that will help you uncover your unconscious biases. Ask your course supervisor or other TAs if there are such workshops or resources available (also see the Additional Resources section for Chapter 4).

Keep in mind that as a TA you're in a position to influence student grades; therefore, you need to be perceived as objective and impartial. You can be personable and friendly, but don't be a friend to your students, and avoid developing personal relationships with them. If you decide to meet a student for coffee, make it clear that this is an open invitation to all students in the class. Avoid situations where you may be perceived as being biased or favouring some students over others. If possible, avoid having a relative or friend in your class; you may need to switch class sections or TA assignments. This may be difficult if you're an undergraduate TA, so you'll have to be careful to avoid the perception of bias toward students you know from other situations. Respect confidences and keep in mind you're in a position of trust. Above all, be aware that your behaviour reflects on the course, program, faculty, and institution.

Scenario 1.3 Your best friend is getting married in Hawaii in two months. You've been asked to be in the wedding party, but the wedding will be in the middle of the term, and you'd have to miss two tutorials that you teach. What should you do?

Scenario 1.4 You've just seen your class list for your lab section and realize that one of the students is your sister's best friend. What should you do?

Scenario 1.5 You're attracted to one of your students, someone who has come back to school after several years in the workforce. You know you can't date a student but would really like to explore a relationship with this person. What should you do?

Checklist: Items to Discuss with the Course Instructor, Supervisor, or Coordinator

◇ **Teaching schedule:** class times and locations; expected time spent before class starts and after class; outside-of-class time requirements such as office hours and meetings with the teaching team.

◇ **Course content:** level of difficulty and learning outcomes.

◇ **Course materials:** print or online, required or recommended?

◇ **Course organization and structure:** lecture, seminars, tutorials, labs, studios, or fieldwork?; number of students in the sections to which you've been assigned.

◇ **Responsibilities in a lecture course:** clarify your role with respect to attendance, assistance with logistics, activities, interactions with students, marking, teaching parts of the lessons.

◇ **Responsibilities in tutorials or seminars:** clarify your role with respect to preparing teaching materials, lesson plans, and assessments.

◇ **Responsibilities in labs or studios:** clarify your role with respect to preparing manuals, instructions, demonstrations, equipment setup, and cleanup.

◇ **Responsibilities in fieldwork or community outreach components:** clarify your role with respect to arranging sessions, transportation, supervision, and evaluation.

◇ **Communication with students:** course policies on method and timing of responses; amount of assistance that is appropriate.

◇ **Student support:** frequency and location of office hours; arranging and participating in review sessions; and campus resources to assist students with academic or personal concerns.

◇ **Marking:** frequency of marking assignments, quizzes, and exams; availability of marking guides and rubrics.

◇ **Course policies:** on late assignments, review of exams and grades, and academic misconduct.

◇ **Responsibilities after classes have ended:** invigilation, marking finals, calculating grades.

◇ **Record keeping:** format for recording attendance (if required), participation, student assessments, assignment of grades.

◇ **Resources to support your teaching:** campus or program-training programs, helpful websites and references, names of experienced TAs who can act as mentors.

Possible Scenario Responses

Scenario 1.1 You've just been notified that you've been assigned to a TA position that starts next week. Of all the many questions you have, which five are the most urgent that you should act on right away?

↓

There are many questions you could ask, such as:

- What will be my role? Will I interact directly or help outside of the class?
- How many hours per week will I be expected to commit to these tasks?
- Are there weeks when I will need to spend more time on TA duties?
- What will be my schedule of duties?
- At what level are the students?
- Is this a required course?

- What resources are available to help me prepare?
- Will we meet (as a group with other TAs or just with the instructor) to prepare for the first lesson (tasks)?

Scenario 1.2 As part of your hours of work, you're expected to set up before each lab and clean up after. You have a class right after the lab ends and must rush off without cleaning up. Your supervisor mentions that you're not doing an adequate job of cleanup. What should you do?

⬇

Explain to your supervisor that you have a class right after (you should not have to be late for your class) and ask if you can clean after your class or if there's something else you could do instead of the cleanup.

Scenario 1.3 Your best friend is getting married in Hawaii in two months. You've been asked to be in the wedding party, but the wedding will be in the middle of the term, and you'd have to miss two tutorials that you teach. What should you do?

⬇

Talk to your course supervisor right away and offer to find a substitute and make a fair exchange for them teaching your classes. Make sure you update the supervisor about the details.

Scenario 1.4 You've just seen your class list for your lab section and realize that one of the students is your sister's best friend. What should you do?

↓

Tell your course supervisor immediately to see if you can switch sessions. If you can't, make sure you're professional and avoid any favouritism or suggestion of favouritism. If possible, have someone else mark the friend's work. If this is not possible, make sure all students' names are hidden before you get the papers for marking.

Scenario 1.5 You're attracted to one of your students, someone who has come back to school after several years in the workforce. You know you can't date a student but would really like to explore a relationship with this person. What should you do?

↓

Avoid any favouritism or suggestion of favouritism. After the marks are submitted and posted, send them flowers and ask them out!

PREPARING FOR YOUR FIRST SESSION

It's common to be excited and a little nervous before your first class. Even experienced instructors get the jitters before the first class each term. There are several steps you can take ahead of time to ease your anxiety and ensure that your class runs smoothly.

BEFORE CLASS

Your course supervisor will usually contact you before classes begin. If they have not, be sure to arrange a meeting to clarify your role in the course and obtain any resources that are available, such as texts, handouts, web links, and so on (see Chapter 1). Identify the learning goals for the course and review the content for the first few classes so you can do some background preparation if there are any gaps in your understanding of the concepts.

Visit the space where you'll be teaching ahead of time. Determine how long it will take you to get to the class so you can arrive a few minutes early. Make sure you know how to use the AV equipment, computers, and other tech provided in the classroom. If you're bringing your own computer, make sure you've installed the necessary hardware. If you'll be teaching in a lab or other practical setting, make sure you know where everything is and check safety protocols and procedures.

HAVE A PLAN

In advance of your interaction with students, prepare a well-organized, detailed outline of what and how you'll be teaching. Effective instructors often prepare this type of lesson plan or a checklist for every class they teach, along with the amount of time they expect to spend on each topic or activity. If you'll be presenting an introduction to a session, short lesson, or complete lecture, see Chapter 3 for insights on how to prepare effective teaching lessons. Visualize how the lesson will go and try to anticipate what might occur at each step. If you'll be giving a lecture or introduction to a practical class or discussion, prepare your talk and practise it in front of a friend, pet, or mirror. You can also record it and play it back. This will help you pace your talk and give you more confidence in front of students. You can rely on your plan to ensure you present all the concepts on time, but be flexible – gauge how students are responding to your instruction and be prepared to modify your plan as needed.

Before your first class, ask your course supervisor any questions or discuss any concerns you have. TAs who have taught the course in the past can also be an excellent resource. If you don't know of anyone, you can ask the course supervisor or instructor to make suggestions.

Scenario 2.1 You're very nervous about the first lab you'll be teaching. You've practised your introduction several times but each time you feel more anxious about what you're going to say as well as how the whole lab will go. What should you do?

FIRST—CLASS INTRODUCTIONS

The first few minutes of your introductory session will set the tone for the whole term. First impressions are important in establishing a positive learning environment. Greet students as they come in with a pleasant smile, ask them for their name and use it to welcome them, and give them instructions on where they can sit. Once the class begins, introduce yourself and give some background, such as where you're from and what you're studying (a few positive words about your own experience in a similar course might be interesting and inspiring for students).

Explain to students how they should communicate with you outside of class. There's a vast variety of media to use, such as emails, discussion boards, and, to a lesser extent, tweeting and Facebook posts. Using institutional emails or course management systems is often recommended. It's usually not a good idea to give out personal phone numbers and emails to your students. Make sure you set boundaries for all electronic communications – for example, let them know the hours when you'll be checking email and how long your response time will generally be. If you're expected to provide support outside of class time, tell students when and where you'll be holding office hours or review sessions.

If you have the time and a small enough class, ask students to introduce themselves and say one or two things about their backgrounds, or have an icebreaker activity. The type of icebreaker you use will depend on the type of class and the amount of time you have for this activity. There are many examples online. Choose one that is appropriate for your situation. Getting to know the students and having them speak up in this first class will reassure them that their contributions will be welcome.

One of the best ways to create a positive atmosphere is to use your students' names often. To facilitate this, give each student a card and ask them to make a name tent (the folded card can sit on their desk), which can include the name they wish to be called in class and their preferred pronouns. If you're worried that you won't remember how to pronounce some names, you may want to record phonetic spellings for your own use. Some institutions have class lists with students' photos; these can help you get to know your students. If you're in a small classroom, lab, studio, seminar, or tutorial where students will sit in the same place each class, make a seating plan and make every effort to call students by name. If the class is small, you can collect the name tents at the end of each class and replace them before the next. In a large class, ask students to bring their name tents each class and bring spare cards for those who forget. This will help you associate names and faces.

Another way to begin fostering an inclusive atmosphere is to set up community guidelines as a part of your introduction to the class. Ask students to contribute guidelines for interacting in class and creating a safe environment that will help them to learn. See Chapter 4 for more details on community guidelines.

Students will appreciate your efforts to learn their names, get to know them, and establish a respectful environment.

EXPLAIN THE PURPOSE OF LESSONS AND FACILITATE ENGAGEMENT

In all classes (not just the first class!), make sure your instructions and explanations are clear. Be transparent about why the information or instructions you're providing will help them successfully complete a learning activity. This will get their attention and will help motivate students and enhance engagement.

Monitor students' expressions to determine whether they seem lost and check in frequently to see if they have questions. You should also ask students questions to gauge their understanding. Be sensitive to students who are shy and offer some way for them to "pass" if they're not comfortable answering a question. When students know what's expected of them and are engaged, they're less likely to be distracted or disruptive in the classroom.

If possible, circulate throughout the class rather than standing in the same place. If students are working in groups, try to spend equal time with each group. If clarification is needed on some aspects of the activity, call the class to attention, summarize the essential information, or provide explanations for common points of confusion.

Check your timeline frequently to be sure you're on schedule. Be aware of what the students are doing: Are they fully engaged, or have they moved on to other activities not related to the course work? You may even take an informal poll to see if students need more time or are ready to move on. Based on the ability of students to complete the work, you can adjust the timing of activities as necessary.

Scenario 2.2 During your first tutorial, you realize that you're behind schedule and will not be able to address all the topics required. What should you do?

AFTER CLASS

Don't expect your classes to be perfect. A good way to keep track of your impressions of lessons is to record them in a teaching journal, either as an electronic file or as written comments in a notebook. You might want to think about and comment on aspects of the class that went well or didn't go well, including delivery of content and timing.

Make a note of anything you need to look up or find answers to before the next class so you can be sure to get back to students. Occasionally, something may come up that you feel your course supervisor should know about (e.g., students would like more practice problems). Communicate these clearly and in a positive manner to the course instructor or coordinator.

Think critically about changes you could make the next time you teach the class. It's often helpful to talk to other TAs or mentors to review how the class went and consider changes for the future.

Scenario 2.3 After reflecting on how your first class went, you realize you made an error in what you told students. What should you do?

Checklist: To-Do's before, during, and after Class

Before
◇ Meet with your course supervisor to obtain course information and clarify roles and expectations.

◇ Review content, as necessary.

◇ Check out the room where you'll be teaching.

◇ Prepare a lesson plan with timelines for each stage of the class.

◇ Visualize how each portion of the class will unfold.

◇ Prepare and practise any material you'll be presenting.

◇ Contact your course supervisor or other TAs if you have major concerns.

During
◇ Establish a positive tone by welcoming students.

◇ Introduce yourself and, if possible, have students introduce themselves or have an icebreaker activity; if appropriate, make name tents and a seating plan so you can call students by name.

◇ Set up community guidelines.

◇ Make sure your instructions and explanations are clear.

◇ Check in frequently with students to see if they have questions on concepts or if they need clarification on instructions.

◇ Get student feedback by asking questions, giving demonstrations, or summarizing.

◇ Check your timeline frequently and adjust if necessary.

After

◇ What worked? Why?

◇ What didn't work? Why?

◇ Were the timing and pace good?

◇ What changes will you make for next time?

◇ Are there any student questions for which you must find answers?

◇ Is there information about the content or student feedback the course instructor or coordinator should be told?

Possible Scenario Responses

Scenario 2.1 You're very nervous about the first lab you'll be teaching. You've practised your introduction several times but each time you feel more anxious about what you're going to say as well as how the whole lab will go. What should you do?

↓

Ask experienced TAs in the course for tips. Ask if you can observe an experienced TA teach before your own class. If you're well prepared, but still nervous when the class begins, this will likely ease once you get to know the students. Meeting new students at the beginning of a course can be energizing.

Scenario 2.2 During your first tutorial, you realize that you're behind schedule and will not be able to address all the topics required. What should you do?

↓

You can tell the students you didn't have time to cover X, but they should read about it and email you if they have any questions. Or you can tell them you didn't have time to cover X, but you'll take a few minutes at the beginning of the next tutorial to answer any questions they may have about that material.

In either case, let your course supervisor know what happened and what you've decided to do.

Think about where you lost time and how you can ensure that it doesn't happen again.

Scenario 2.3 After reflecting on how your first class went, you realize you made an error in what you told students. What should you do?

⬇

If it was a minor error and won't affect their work before the next class, you could wait and announce it at the start of the next class. If it was a major error and could have ramifications for their work before the next class, you should consider sending out an email to all students, posting an announcement on the course management system or, if necessary, asking the course instructor to make an announcement at the beginning of class.

DESIGNING LESSONS AND LEARNING ACTIVITIES

You may have the opportunity to design some learning activities. This could be a whole lecture or an activity that is part of a lecture, lab, tutorial, or seminar. The activities should always be developed and aligned with intended learning outcomes and assessments of student learning. If you're going to be teaching a course on your own, you'll need to consider the goals of the course, the content or required course material, the schedule of the session, and the options for assessing student learning. The following suggestions can be used for a learning activity or lesson or expanded to cover an entire course.

LEARNING OUTCOMES AND OBJECTIVES

Learning outcomes (LOs) are one-sentence descriptions of what students should learn from or be able to do after the lesson. Whereas learning outcomes focus on what the student will gain, learning objectives describe the intentions of the instructor when designing a lesson. When writing outcomes, it's helpful to use the SMART approach: outcomes should be Specific, Measurable, Attainable, Relevant, and Timely. A good way to start an outcome is with a phrase like this: "By the end of this lesson (activity, etc.), students should be able to ..." This format can be applied to any aspect of learning, such as a course, lecture, lab, tutorial, seminar, or single activity. Devising explicit LOs will guide you in developing the structure of your lesson and provide students with a clear description of what they're expected to learn.

When writing learning outcomes, it's important to consider the level at which you expect the students to learn and work with information, concepts, and skills. Bloom and colleagues (1956) proposed a hierarchy of cognitive or thinking skills, ranging from the lowest order (remembering information) to the highest (evaluating information). Modifications of Bloom's hierarchy have been developed, but the original scale of lower to higher cognitive skills is still commonly used (see Table 1). When writing LOs, decide the level at which you want students to understand the material; for example, do you want them to comprehend, analyze, or evaluate? Then choose verbs for the LO that relate to the cognitive level you've identified. The verbs you use in your LO will directly align with your assessment of student learning. You'll find a link to a more comprehensive list of verbs associated with each thinking skill in the Additional Resources section for this chapter.

Table 1 Bloom's levels of cognition and associated verbs

	Thinking skills	Example verbs
Higher order ↑	Evaluation	Judge, test, critique, defend, criticize
	Synthesis (creating)	Design, build, construct, plan, produce, devise, invent
	Analysis	Categorize, examine, organize, compare/contrast
	Application	Use, diagram, graph, draw, apply, solve, calculate, construct
	Comprehension (understanding)	Interpret, summarize, explain, infer, discuss
Lower order	Knowledge (remembering)	List, find, name, identify, locate, describe, define

An example of a knowledge-based learning outcome for a class in human anatomy studying tendons could be "By the end of this lesson, students will be able to *identify* the tendons in the human hand and foot." A similar example for a classical studies course on Ancient Greece could be "By the end of this class, students will be able to *name* three sites of importance in Ancient Greece." If you expect students to achieve the higher level of analysis, an example LO would be "By the end of this unit, students will be able to *compare* the function of tendons in the hand with those in the foot." In the classical studies course, a LO at the same level would be "By the end of the semester, students will be able to *contrast* the relative importance of the three ancient Greek sites." At the higher level of synthesis, you may have LOs such as "By the end of the course, students will be able to *redesign* the placement of tendons to improve the function of the hand" or "By the end of the term, students will be able to *design* a perfect temple complex that would meet the needs of ancient Greeks." These LOs describe what you expect students to be able to accomplish; your assessments, whether tests, exams, or projects, should align with the LOs.

Once you've determined your learning outcomes, decide what examples and learning activities you'll incorporate and how much time you'll spend on each LO. Try to engage students as much as possible, e.g., by using active learning techniques (see below).

Scenario 3.1 In your course, one learning outcome is for students to "understand the basis of Norse gods." How could you improve the wording, so it's a clear learning outcome?

PLANNING A LESSON

Backward design is a useful process in developing a lesson. First, consider what you expect students to demonstrate. Will they be able to recite certain information, describe certain concepts, perform a skill, or evaluate material? In other words, determine the learning outcomes for the lesson. Next, determine what information needs to be provided – either through lecture presentations, assigned pre-class readings, group presentations, or a variety of other means – to help your students achieve the LOs.

Start the lesson or class with interesting information that will capture students' attention and provide the rationale for the lesson. Consider what activities could help to reinforce comprehension of the concepts and accomplishment of the learning outcomes. An engaging lecture may be sufficient, but group discussions may be more effective. Be realistic about the amount of time you have in class for each component of the lesson in your plan but be prepared to make changes to the time allocation if necessary.

You'll also need to consider how effective the lesson and activities are in assisting students to achieve the learning outcomes. In addition to observing how students respond to the lesson, you may want to include an informal assessment. For example, toward the end of class, you can ask for a summary of group discussions or ask students a series of review questions. You'll find other suggestions for assessing student learning in Chapter 7.

Scenario 3.2 The class has been fully engaged in the discussion, and you have another activity planned. However, there are only ten minutes left in the class. What can you do?

ACTIVE LEARNING

Teaching techniques at postsecondary institutions have traditionally been formal lectures and seminars. However, studies have shown that student performance improves when students actively engage with course information and concepts (e.g., Freeman et al. 2014).

There are many ways to integrate active learning into your lessons, ranging from simple techniques that are easy to incorporate to more complex activities that require considerable preparation:

◇ Ask students to respond to questions or surveys by raising their hands or submitting their answers using a personal response system (PRS) (sometimes called clickers) or cellphone.

◇ Think-pair-share is a technique where students are asked a question; for a minute or two they individually prepare an answer; they discuss their answer with a neighbouring student; and, finally, they share with the whole class.

◇ Group- or team-based activities require students to individually prepare for the activity before they come to class (there may be a quiz to start). Then, in class, students work in teams to complete activities such as filling in worksheets requiring answers to questions, problem solving, working through case studies, producing concept maps, and so on.

◇ The jigsaw method is a more elaborate form of group work. Typically, students work on a case study or multifaceted problem. Each student in a home group becomes an "expert" on a different aspect of the case by working with other students assigned to the same aspect. Students then return to their home group and contribute what they've learned to help solve the problem or prepare a stance on the case study.

◇ Send-a-problem involves students writing a question and appropriate answer on a notecard, which is then sent to multiple groups to discuss and revise the question and answer, as necessary.

◇ The snowball technique is a fun method where students write the answer to a question on a piece of paper, crumple it into a "snowball" and throw it across the room. Everyone picks up a snowball and throws it again. Finally, each student picks up a snowball, and this time reads the answer aloud when called upon (this preserves anonymity).

◇ One-minute paper activities require students to write down something confusing (also known as the "muddiest point") or noteworthy and submit it to the instructor; this can then help guide subsequent activities.

Another activity that can promote engagement and reflection is called "double journal entry." Students take notes as usual on one side of the page and write reflections or notes to themselves on the other side as they review their class material.

When choosing an activity to include in your lesson, consider the intended outcome, the time required, and the restraints of the classroom itself. Whether the activity is embedded in a lecture, tutorial, seminar, or lab, be sure to close the circle by summarizing the main points to reinforce the relevance of the activity to the lesson.

Scenario 3.3 You're going to be teaching a tutorial on a topic, and you remember from last year that it was not an engaging lesson. What strategies could you incorporate into your lesson to make it more engaging?

Scenario 3.4 Your class is quiet, and several students are hesitant about participating in activities. Which activities could you use to encourage participation by all students?

Checklist: Designing Learning Activities

◇ Decide what you want students to learn from the lesson or activity.

◇ Identify the level of cognition at which you want students to understand the material in the lesson or activity.

◇ Use the SMART approach to prepare student outcomes (choose the verbs to align with the depth of learning and skills you expect).

◇ Choose a lesson design or activity that will satisfy learning outcomes.

◇ Decide how you'll determine if students have achieved proficiency with the desired outcomes, that is, choose an appropriate means of assessment.

Possible Scenario Responses

Scenario 3.1 In your course, one learning outcome is for students to "understand the basis of Norse gods." How could you improve the wording, so it's a clear learning outcome?

↓

The word *understand* is vague, so it should be replaced with a specific verb, which will depend on what you want the student to be able to do with this information. You also need a timeline (end of this class, end of this section, etc.). For example, you could use, "By the end of this class, students will be able to describe the origins of the three main Norse gods."

Scenario 3.2 The class has been fully engaged in the discussion, and you have another activity planned. However, there are only ten minutes left in the class. What would you do?

↓

It's important to come full circle and summarize the work students have completed. Consult with the course instructor and if there is time in the next class, continue with the new activity then. This can be a review or reinforcement of the concepts presented in the previous class.

Scenario 3.3 You're going to be teaching a tutorial on a topic and you remember from last year that it was not an engaging lesson. What strategies could you incorporate into your lesson to make it more engaging?

↓

You should review the learning outcomes for the tutorial and confirm that they're clear to the students. If students know what's expected, they'll be more attentive. Then consider various active learning techniques, such as discussing questions in small groups, preparing a set of questions students can answer with clickers, or asking students to draw out steps or draw diagrams. Once you have a plan, meet with the course instructor. Explain your reasons for wanting to change the lesson; outline what you would like to do and how it will fit into the time allocated. Ask your supervisor for feedback and suggestions. Hopefully, they'll be supportive!

Scenario 3.4 Your class is very quiet and several students are hesitant about participating in activities. Which activities could you use to encourage participation by all students?

↓

Any activity where responses can be anonymous – for example, the snowball activity is a good choice. Asking students to "think-pair-share" or work in groups to encourage participation before answering can also be effective.

CREATING AN INCLUSIVE LEARNING ENVIRONMENT

Whether you're teaching a lecture, tutorial, lab, or leading a discussion, you'll likely find your class wonderfully diverse. Students in your class may have different academic and cultural backgrounds. They may be of similar or diverse ages, and, in some cases, you may have an imbalance of genders. As instructors, we often make assumptions about students and have unconscious biases. It's important that we become aware of our biases and whether they're based on race, religion, cultural background, gender, or privilege. Identifying your biases, avoiding stereotyping, and developing an open and accepting attitude are not easy and will take considerable effort. Find out if there are diversity, equity, and inclusion training sessions or workshops at your institution and, if possible, attend some to help you become aware of and overcome your biases. Students and your course supervisor will likely have their own biases; a respectful and objective approach to situations where biases are evident will help you avoid insensitive interactions. Creating an inclusive learning environment means that everyone will be treated with respect, will feel safe, and will be valued as learners.

ESTABLISH A RESPECTFUL AND SAFE SPACE

Always be personable: smile and welcome your students to class. There are additional steps, some of which were mentioned in Chapter 2, that you can take to build an inclusive environment.

Set up community guidelines. Ask students to provide suggestions for interacting in class and creating a safe environment that will help them to learn. Students often list things such as "respecting others," "listening when others are speaking," and "making an effort to participate." You can add items of your own and have a few examples ready in case the class hesitates to contribute (e.g., arrive on time, respect the opinions of others, participate fully, and encourage others to participate). Remember to thank students for their suggestions and ask if anyone has anything more to add before closing the discussion. Remind students of these guidelines each class, either by showing a slide at the beginning or making a poster and displaying it prominently. Each time you refer to the guidelines, ask if there's anything they would like to add.

Students need to know that they're recognized as individuals who are expected to contribute to class discussions and that their contributions are valued. Get to know students' names and use names and preferred pronouns during discussions or when you ask questions; if possible, move around the classroom as you interact with groups of students. Students are more likely to respect your teaching efforts if they know they are seen as individuals who are encouraged to contribute to the classroom community.

Be aware of your communication style and how it may be perceived by students. Make sure your intentions are clear and avoid what may be interpreted as inappropriate, culturally specific references or humour. Use gender-neutral pronouns such as *they* or *them*. Ensure your salutations, examples, questions, and anecdotes are culturally neutral (e.g., instead of saying, "Have a great Christmas," you could say, "Have a great holiday" or "Have a great break"). Welcome questions or visitors to your office hours warmly, with a smile. If you're not sure how to respond in a particular situation, it may be helpful to ask yourself, "How would I like to be treated if I were the student in this situation?"

If you've taken care to create a respectful environment for students, you should expect respect in return for your efforts in helping them learn.

Scenario 4.1 Several students sit together in a large class and frequently talk and share media posts during your lesson. They appear to be oblivious to your lecture or that you're giving important instructions. What would you do?

RESPECT STUDENTS' TIME CONSTRAINTS

Model appropriate behaviours and always start on time. If you regularly begin on time and start with important instructions, students will know it's in their best interests to be punctual. Use specific cues that students recognize when you're beginning the class or want to get their attention during class activities. Finish on time, even if you need to bring your lesson to a close before you planned. Most students will have classes after yours and will need time to get to their next class on time.

Be mindful of the time and effort you're expecting of students; remember that they have other courses. Try to spread out assignments and quizzes if possible and provide due dates well in advance. You can be sympathetic to complaints that they have too much work for a particular day, but most of the time, due dates will be beyond your control. Remind students about upcoming due dates to help them budget their time.

Scenario 4.2 On the first day of class, you informed students that you'll be starting on time and that you expect them to be ready for the lesson. Yet each day you have a few students who arrive ten, fifteen, or even thirty minutes late. What would you do?

ENHANCE PARTICIPATION AND STUDENT LEARNING

Some students may not wish to contribute to class discussions even though they have relevant ideas or know answers to your questions. Having students work in pairs or small groups gives all students a chance to have their voices heard without speaking in front of the class. Working in groups also provides students with an opportunity to learn from one another and for the TA to work with each group. With time, shy or introverted students may relax and contribute more to class discussions; be patient, as this may take time. See Chapter 5 for more information on assigning students to groups and effective group work.

Not all students learn the same way, so use a variety of techniques when you explain concepts or ideas. Diagrams can be useful for some students but confusing for others. Be prepared to provide explanations in alternative ways (e.g., orally or using text, images, diagrams, and videos). Try different strategies with students who are having difficulties (you may notice blank faces, a lack of success in their work, or their questions may suggest they're struggling) until you find an approach that is effective for most of them.

If a student has difficulties completing classroom activities, they may be facing challenges that are not obvious, such as physical limitations, learning disabilities, or emotional struggles that may be a result of one or more equity issues related to their class, race, or gender. For example, financial obstacles may act as a barrier to completing coursework. Some students need to work to put themselves through school, and this can influence their performance. Or a student who is experiencing distress because of discrimination they are encountering inside or outside the classroom may be struggling to meet their assignment deadlines. Physical impairments may be apparent to you, but conditions such as mental or physiological health and equity issues are less obvious.

Approach students privately with your concerns about their progress and ask if modifications would help them complete the course work. Students are sometimes reluctant to admit that they're having difficulties. If you find out they have challenges or extenuating circumstances, you can suggest they talk to your institution's centre for accessible learning and inclusion. If they're willing to accept modifications to your teaching, discuss this with your course supervisor before devising alternative activities. For example, if a student is unable to attend a field trip, the supervisor may have images and videos with commentary that can be posted so the student can participate virtually. If students receive formal concessions from your institution's accessibility and inclusion centre, gracefully acknowledge the situation and ensure the accommodations are met (you may have to discuss how to create suitable modifications with the course supervisor). Respect the student's confidentiality and discuss all actions privately.

PROVIDE POSITIVE SUPPORT

When students volunteer to ask or answer questions in class, be positive and encouraging. Students are sensitive to responses to their questions; they're leery of looking foolish in front of their peers. Thank them for their contribution, even if their answer is incomplete and others add to it. Do not judge students if they lack sufficient preparation from previous courses; instead, provide all students with resources for background information. You can present this information in a positive way as "refresher" material. Avoid criticizing a student's response in front of others; if necessary, you can take a student aside and ask to speak to them after class to clarify misconceptions. Also, to avoid the perception of having favourites, don't single out students for lavish praise.

Of course, if at any time a situation arises that makes you uncomfortable, or if you're anxious about a student's or your own well-being, don't hesitate to talk to your course supervisor.

Scenario 4.3 You have several students in your tutorial who know the material but are not comfortable expressing themselves in English. Participation during the tutorials counts for marks, and you're concerned that they'll not do as well as they should. What would you do?

Scenario 4.4 You're teaching a lab where students work in groups. One of your groups consists of four students who share the same first language, which is not English. During the lab, they often speak in their first language, which is a problem because you don't know if they're on task, experiencing difficulty, or possibly conducting unsafe procedures. What would you do?

Scenario 4.5 You identify as female. In conversation with your male colleagues, you realize that compared to them, some of your students contact you more frequently and outside of your designated hours. You're concerned that your students have different expectations of you because you're female. What can you do to ensure that this is not the case?

Checklist: Creating an Inclusive Learning Environment

◇ Examine your own unconscious biases (e.g., by attending a training session) and take steps to overcome them.

◇ Set up community guidelines the first day; refer to them each class and add items over time.

◇ Call your students by name and preferred pronoun. Use name tents or a seating plan.

◇ Be clear, culturally neutral, and avoid inappropriate references or humour.

◇ Have students work in pairs or small groups and change the composition of groups regularly, if appropriate.

◇ Spread out assignments and quizzes if possible and provide due dates well in advance.

◇ Use a variety of teaching techniques in your explanations.

◇ Be supportive when students require accommodations.

◇ Be positive and encouraging when students volunteer to ask or answer questions in class.

◇ Provide resources as refresher materials for the entire class to fill in preparation gaps among some students.

◇ Do not single out students for criticism or praise.

◇ Consult with your course supervisor if you're concerned about a student's well-being or are not sure how to handle a situation.

Possible Scenario Responses

Scenario 4.1 Several students sit together in a large class and frequently talk and share media posts during your lesson. They appear to be oblivious to your lecture or that you're giving important instructions. What would you do?

↓

During your lecture or before you give instructions, indicate the importance of the information you're providing. Students may be half-listening; this will cue them to pay full attention. Remind students that they all agreed to the community guidelines, which hopefully include being respectful when others are speaking. If the talking is disruptive, you may wish to stop giving instructions. The silence will alert them that their voices are the only ones being heard, and they'll stop. Alternatively, ask another TA or a colleague to sit near the students during class. The students may change their behaviour if they realize someone of authority will take notice.

Another option is to talk to one or more of the students (after class) and let them know that their behaviour is disruptive to students around them. Ask them to hold off sharing their posts until after class.

Scenario 4.2 On the first day of class, you informed students that you'll be starting on time and that you expect them to be ready for the lesson. Yet each day you have a few students who arrive ten, fifteen, or even thirty minutes late. What would you do?

↓

Continue to start on time as initially stated. Remind students that everyone agreed to the community guidelines, which hopefully include arriving to class on time. You may wish to talk to the students that tend to arrive late individually. Ask them why they're having difficulties arriving on time. There could be a valid reason (late buses, a previous class across campus). If appropriate, provide some suggestions as to how they can get to class earlier.

Scenario 4.3 You have several students in your tutorial who know the material but are not comfortable expressing themselves in English. Participation during the tutorials counts for marks, and you're concerned that they'll not do as well as they should. What would you do?

↓

Try having them discuss things in small groups and report back to the class. They can take turns reporting to the whole group when they're more comfortable.

Assign roles within groups – for example, recorder, reporter. They'll eventually perform all the roles.

Scenario 4.4 You're teaching a lab where students work in groups. One of your groups consists of four students who share the same first language, which is not English. During the lab, they often speak in their first language, which is a problem because you don't know if they're on task, experiencing difficulty, or possibly conducting unsafe procedures. What would you do?

↓

Explain the need to speak English in class as a safety concern and so you can assess where they are with the assigned tasks. If you hear them speaking in another language, always gently remind them that they should be speaking English in class.

Scenario 4.5 You identify as female. In conversation with your male colleagues, you realize that compared to them, some of your students contact you more frequently and outside of your designated hours. You're concerned that your students have different expectations for you because you're female. What can you do to ensure that this is not the case?

↓

Set clear guidelines and expectations at the beginning of the term and be consistent with all students. Remind students (kindly) of your hours. You can even have an automatic response that will tell students when you'll reply. However, if one student repeatedly asks for extra help outside designated hours, ask the student (privately) if there's a reason why they're always contacting you when they do. There could be some issues you're not aware of – for example, concerning work or family – and you may have to work this out with the student.

FACILITATING CLASSROOM INTERACTION

Discussions with students – either in small groups, during seminars, or one on one – can provide a wealth of information on student thinking and learning. Facilitating these dialogues is a skill that takes practice. Knowing what questions to ask is the first step. Having suitable responses to students' ideas is also key to effective facilitation.

USING QUESTIONS EFFECTIVELY

Use student responses to your questions to gauge whether you need to review material you thought students understood or whether you can introduce more sophisticated information to continue building on concepts.

How you phrase these questions will depend on your intentions. The questions you ask can take a variety of forms: they can be open-ended (i.e., students need to think and make connections) or close-ended (i.e., you're expecting a single correct answer). Both can be useful.

If you want to check that students have the necessary background knowledge, a closed-ended question would be appropriate. For example, you could ask, "What is the molecule that is used to transport energy in the cell?" But if you want students to apply knowledge, propose new ideas, or evaluate information, then open-ended questions would be more appropriate. You could ask, "Would you expect oxygen availability to influence cell function? Why?" If you want students to respond to your questions, avoid using rhetorical questions such as "Isn't energy transport in cells awesome?" Think carefully about how you phrase questions and prepare them before the lesson, targeting those concepts that you expect students to find challenging. It's difficult to devise good questions during a lesson and much easier to modify questions you've already prepared.

Give students enough time to think about the question, especially more challenging questions, so they can prepare an answer. Be patient and wait at least ten seconds (sing "Happy Birthday" to yourself – silently). Explain to students beforehand how you want them to respond to specific questions. Do you want them to shout out answers or raise their hands, or will you randomly choose students to respond (cold-calling)? Be careful with cold-calling, as some students may find it intimidating or stressful, especially in large classes. If you do call on students, give them the option to pass if they don't have an answer they're willing to share.

In large classes, students can respond to multiple-choice questions using coded cards (e.g., each student has cards labelled *A* to *E,* and they hold up the card that corresponds to their chosen answer). You and the instructor can see their responses, but other students are less likely to. In some classrooms, it might be possible to use personal-response or polling systems (clickers, cell phones) to submit answers. An alternative to requiring students to respond individually is to have them discuss the question in pairs or small groups before volunteering a response or inputting a choice electronically.

Carefully structured questions can be used to guide students' thoughts on a topic. This helps them practise developing a logical progression of ideas toward a solution, and it will build their confidence.

Scenario 5.1 You asked an open-ended question that you thought was straightforward, but no one responds. What would you do?

Scenario 5.2 When a student who regularly sits near the front consistently responds to your questions, the other students stop offering responses. What would you do?

Scenario 5.3 A student responds to a question with a comment that does not apply to the topic of discussion. What would you do?

LEADING GROUP DISCUSSIONS

Your goal should be for all students in the group or class to participate and contribute their ideas. Before you start, create an environment where all students' ideas are respected and review the code of conduct or guidelines students have prepared for working together as a group. Help students get to know one another (see Chapters 2 and 3).

To encourage interaction and participation, arrange the physical space so that all participants can see one another and so the facilitator is part of the group (not sitting behind a desk or separate from the circle of students). Give all students equal attention and avoid looking at any one student more than others. Clearly describe the topic or problem to be discussed. Let students know that you expect all students to participate and explain how participation contributes to their course grades.

Questions are an integral part of tutorials or seminars where students learn through discussion. Several elements contribute to effective discussions. As at the beginning of a lesson, start with a bridge or "hook," such as an anecdote or comment that will capture their interest. Then, present the focus or question of the discussion, the objective, and what students should be able to do following the discussion. Determine what students already know about the topic by asking questions or giving them a short quiz. You can then begin the discussion of your topic with a series of questions directed at different students to facilitate the participation of all. As you bring the discussion to a close, either you or one of the students should summarize the main points that emerged. Be sure to thank participants for their contributions.

When managing student discussions, be respectful if students are apprehensive about sharing their ideas. Student participation can sometimes be slow initially. Start with questions that are easy to answer, giving everyone a chance to participate. Gradually ask more challenging questions that require them to express opinions or synthesize ideas; welcome different opinions or ideas about a topic. Be objective and conciliatory in the way you handle conflicting ideas. Paraphrase their ideas to underscore similarities and respectfully address differences; students can be sensitive to put-downs. Take steps to ensure arguments don't evolve into personal attacks.

Scenario 5.4 You've managed to excite the interest of your students on a topic that you planned to discuss only briefly. Yet they continue to ask very good questions about the topic. What would you do?

Scenario 5.5 During a discussion, two students strongly disagree on an issue. What would you do?

Scenario 5.6 You've prepared a series of questions for students to discuss in pairs or small groups. The students are fully engaged in their group discussion, but it's time to summarize the main points of this activity and you're finding it difficult to get their attention. How could you effectively get students' attention and reinforce the learning outcomes of this activity?

Scenario 5.7 During a class discussion, there was no clear answer to your question and students became frustrated. What would you do?

CREATING EFFECTIVE GROUPS

Educational research suggests that group work enhances student learning for all participants, and yet students often resist the assignment of group work. When introducing the group activity, it's important to explicitly state the value of learning to work cooperatively for students' future careers.

Arranging and managing groups of students to work together effectively to complete learning activities can be challenging. In a large lecture room, it's easiest to have students self-select who they'll work with in a group, typically those students that sit close by. In smaller classes, students can be randomly assigned to groups by having them number off (e.g., one to six, if you'll have six groups). If you want to influence and balance the composition of each group, you can assign students nonrandomly, based on gender, grades, and/ or cultural background, to promote a diversity of perspectives. If possible, change the composition of the groups from time to time to allow students to work with and get to know different classmates during the course. This may not always be appropriate for long-term projects, but if group management challenges arise, this can be a way to deal with personality issues.

Design the group activity to be relevant, interesting, and challenging in the sense that more than one person needs to be involved to complete the work. Motivate students to work effectively together by including both an individual and group component in the assessment. We also recommend that a portion of student grades be based on peer assessment.

Students need to get to know one another, including their strengths and weaknesses. They should then determine what procedural roles (discussion lead, reporter or recorder, communication lead) each member can carry out. During a long-term project, students can rotate through these roles. Help the groups develop guidelines on how to work together.

Ensure that students have the time and the space to work together face to face. Arrange for breakout rooms if students are working in a virtual environment. Some class time must be dedicated to group organization and work, especially if students commute and have full schedules. Students must agree on how the group will communicate outside of class. Be sure that you also have their contact information in case you need to facilitate communication among group members. Groups should also set timelines for the completion of each step of the project or activity. You should check in with groups regularly to guide discussions, get an update on their progress, and determine if there are issues that require your intervention.

Scenario 5.8 In a group of four, one student tends to dominate, discounting the suggestions of others and setting the tasks for the other group members. One student approaches you and explains that they feel uncomfortable in this group. What would you do?

Scenario 5.9 One student in the group is always in a hurry to get through the activity. Their tasks are left incomplete, and they socialize instead, talking about topics not related to the project. What would you do?

Scenario 5.10 In a group of four, one student is shy and reluctant to voice their ideas or opinions. As a result, two students take over and direct the assignment of tasks and the conceptual content of the project. The fourth student avoids participating, often coming late to group meetings and not completing their portion of the work on time. What would you do?

Checklist: Facilitating Discussions

◇ Establish rules for the constructive and respectful sharing of ideas. Refer to community guidelines the class agreed on during your first meeting.

◇ Explain your expectations for student participation in the discussion.

◇ Survey students for their background knowledge of the topic. Provide interesting background information or context for the discussion.

◇ Present the question to be discussed clearly.

◇ Begin the discussion with questions that are easy to answer.

◇ Ask leading or more challenging questions to guide the discussion.

◇ Acknowledge the value of the contribution of each student.

◇ Paraphrase answers that may not be clear or where the relevance to the discussion is not obvious.

◇ Summarize the main points of the discussion.

Checklist: Creating Effective Groups

◇ Decide ahead of time how you'll assign students to groups (e.g., random, self-select, nonrandom).

◇ Design group activities appropriately; they should be relevant and challenging.

◇ Provide students with the opportunity to come up with guidelines for working as a group.

◇ Make sure learning outcomes, student roles, and expectations for the activity are clear.

◇ If the students will be working in groups on a longer-term project, set timelines, allow sufficient class time for groups to organize themselves, and decide how they'll communicate outside of class.

◇ Have a system to check with groups to make sure they're on time and on task.

Possible Scenario Responses

Scenario 5.1 You asked an open-ended question that you thought was straightforward, but no one responds. What would you do?

↓

Revise the wording of your question and perhaps break it down into a series of questions students can answer more easily. Alternatively, you can ask one of the students to paraphrase your question or tell the class what they think you were asking.

Scenario 5.2 When a student who regularly sits near the front consistently responds to your questions, the other students stop offering responses. What would you do?

↓

You could acknowledge that this student has something to contribute but ask if someone else would like to answer the question. You could ask for a response from a certain sector of the classroom or someone that has not yet responded that day. You may wish to talk to the helpful student privately, letting them know that you appreciate their responses but that you want to allow other students to answer questions. Finally, you could perhaps limit the number of responses per class from this student.

Scenario 5.3 A student responds to a question with a comment that does not apply to the topic of discussion. What would you do?

↓

If possible, paraphrase the response so that it addresses the topic. Acknowledge that the student's comment addresses a related issue but not the topic directly and then ask if they can revise their comment or have something to add about the topic itself.

Scenario 5.4 You've managed to excite the interest of your students on a topic that you planned to discuss only briefly. Yet they continue to ask very good questions about the topic. What would you do?

↓

First, acknowledge their interest. Then offer to set aside another time to continue the discussion or answer their questions through other means (online discussion board, emails) and perhaps provide information to answer some of their questions (links to relevant websites). You must follow through with whatever you have agreed to do. Be sure to address the issue in a subsequent class to see if their interest has been satisfied.

Scenario 5.5 During a discussion, two students strongly disagree on an issue. What would you do?

↓

Paraphrase the stance of each student and identify the merits of each opinion. Try to be objective. If this is a controversial issue, leave it to the students to make up their own minds. If a student expresses an opinion that is not acceptable, such as a racist or misogynist comment, don't shut down the conversation, which can leave students of colour or women alone to grapple with the problem. Instead, see this as a learning opportunity for all your students, and hold the student who made the comment accountable by making it clear that saying x to or about y is not acceptable. Challenge the student to think about how their statements affect others.

Scenario 5.6 You've prepared a series of questions for students to discuss in pairs or small groups. The students are fully engaged in their group discussion, but it's time to summarize the main points of this activity and you're finding it difficult to get their attention. How could you effectively get students' attention and reinforce the learning outcomes of this activity?

↓

Before you give them the topic to discuss, set a time limit and tell them what you expect them to complete. Let them know that you'll ask random groups or pairs to report on their discussions. Have a way to indicate the time they have left for discussion and a signal for students to turn their focus back to the instructor (e.g., a gong, lights off and on, a whistle, clapping, or maracas). Then say, "Thank you for your discussion. This is an important topic."

Scenario 5.7 During a class discussion, there was no clear answer to your question and students became frustrated. What would you do?

↓

Address student frustration either in class, through a discussion board, or in the following class. If appropriate, provide students with an acceptable answer to your question. If there's no clear answer, explain why not along with the value of discussion and differences of opinion in these cases.

Scenario 5.8 In a group of four, one student tends to dominate, discounting the suggestions of others and setting the tasks for the other group members. One student approaches you and explains that they feel uncomfortable in this group. What would you do?

↓

Find out from this student what's specifically making them uncomfortable. Then interact with the entire group, asking each student for their thoughts on the tasks, modelling an inclusive approach to group work. Acknowledge the suggestions of the dominant student but reinforce the need for everyone to contribute. If necessary, you may wish to speak with the dominant student separately after class to get their perspective on the group dynamic and provide them with some advice on effective group work.

Scenario 5.9 One student in the group is always in a hurry to get through the activity. Their tasks are left incomplete, and they socialize instead, talking about other topics not related to the project. What would you do?

↓

Initially, you may want to point out to the student that work still needs to be completed to a group-established standard. This student may have other priorities and not be highly motivated to perform well in the course. You can speak with the student after class to determine what they're willing to contribute to the group effort. Make them appreciate that they have a responsibility to their group and that effective group work is an important skill to learn. Consider a peer assessment of individual contributions to the project. This could motivate the student to be more engaged in the tasks.

Scenario 5.10 In a group of four, one student is shy and reluctant to voice their ideas or opinions. As a result, two students take over and direct the assignment of tasks and the conceptual content of the project. The fourth student avoids participating, often coming late to group meetings and not completing their portion of the work on time. What would you do?

↓

Speak with the group and reinforce that all members of the group need to contribute to the project. Ask them to develop a plan or list of tasks that needs to be completed and, if necessary, facilitate how to assign these tasks. Separately, encourage the shy student to be more forceful in expressing their opinions. Also, talk to the student that comes late to group meetings. Ask why they're having difficulties in contributing. There may be issues that are beyond their control, and perhaps they should reconsider how they can best contribute to the project. Require group members to assess the contributions of each member of the project.

TEACHING WITH TECHNOLOGY

Today's classrooms have a variety of technological aids to assist and increase engagement in lectures, seminars, tutorials, and labs. PowerPoint slides and notes can be enhanced visually by adding images, videos, and animations. Personal response systems (PRSs) or clickers and cellphones can be used to survey students or solicit answers to questions. Students can discuss their answers with other students, which can increase engagement and provide immediate feedback to instructors and students on their understanding of concepts.

Make sure you're familiar with the technology that you'll be required to use. If possible, practise several times so you'll be successful at setting up and accessing any software you'll use while teaching. If you're linking to a website, be sure the link is active and that you can reach it easily. Preview any videos and make sure the content and length are appropriate. If possible, fast-forward to or bookmark the part you want to emphasize. If it's a longer video, it may be helpful to provide students with a list of guiding questions, so they remain focused.

If you're using a PRS or polling system, there are limitations to the type of answers students can provide. For example, they may be limited to choosing one of five possible responses to a multiple-choice question, or they may be able to input short written or numerical answers. One benefit of using this technology is that you can see the number of responses entered and then view a graph of them, which can be used to focus the discussion. Why did students choose one answer over another? The discussion can identify misconceptions which contributed to their incorrect responses.

In most cases, you'll be assisting the instructor with their questions, but you may have the opportunity to design some questions yourself. If so, think about the questions you'll ask: Is the question for review, discussion, or to assess understanding and misconceptions of a concept? Word the questions carefully so they're clear and not too complicated. Decide ahead of time if you'll give a mark for correctness or for participation or both. Don't have too many questions in a single session and make sure to allow enough time for students to answer each question and for general discussion.

In addition to in-class instruction, virtual lessons can be delivered through a variety of meeting platforms or posted on course websites or YouTube. Meeting platforms, such as Zoom, are synchronous;

they allow some interaction with students. Posting platforms, by contrast, are asynchronous and static; they are a good vehicle for providing information and instructions that can be accessed by students at their convenience. Be aware that meetings on online platforms can be hacked and modifications can be made to the visual materials.

Course management systems (e.g., Canvas, Moodle) typically have a variety of functions. In addition to using them to post course materials and resources, they can be used to arrange group activities, deliver and submit assignments, mark student work, give feedback, and post individualized grade books. Discuss your responsibilities within the management system with your course supervisor and make sure you're familiar with the technology and how to use it effectively.

TEACHING ONLINE

Some courses are designed to be offered completely online. If you're teaching an online class in real time, many aspects of teaching in person can be translated into the virtual experience. Students can participate by annotating the slides or whiteboards you're using, adding comments, drawings, emoji, and so on.

You can divide students into small groups by assigning them to virtual breakout rooms so they can discuss topics and work on problem sets. It's always helpful to provide an accessible copy of the breakout-room activity instructions (e.g., a slide with written instructions, a link to Google slides, or written instructions in the chat window) since details can easily be missed. If you provide a Google Doc or other file for students to record their discussion, their work can be shared with the whole class later. As with any group work, it helps to remind students to assign themselves different roles when they're working in a group (e.g., leader or facilitator, recorder, reporter) so they can be more efficient in completing the task.

In addition, you can create virtual-friendly activities that require student participation. For example, you can create documents such as PowerPoint slides with animations that students must activate (click) to progress through problems. You can use websites such as Yoscenario to develop branching-scenario problem sets and online tools such as Educaplay to develop (or share previously created) interactive review games. You can use Slack, which offers chat rooms that can be organized by topic or private groups. All these options are an excellent way to actively engage students in small-group breakout-room exercises.

New programs and platforms are constantly being developed; your institution may indicate which options are acceptable. If that's the case, it will be a matter of choosing the ones that best fit the course objectives while respecting the privacy and confidentiality of students.

Student participation in an online classroom can be facilitated so all students have an opportunity to ask and answer questions. Shy students may prefer to use the public chat or direct-message feature to communicate with others, or they may be more inclined to share by answering poll questions. One added benefit of using polls or surveys is that they can be used to track student participation. Students can also contribute in class using their microphone or chat feature, which can provide a record of student involvement that can be translated into participation marks. These tools are important for motivating students to engage in class. In online classes, it's easier for students to avoid participating for a variety of reasons. Effective use of these tools can help instructors keep track of a student's engagement.

Scenario 6.1 You're a TA in a large lecture section. The instructor has informed you that they'll be using clickers regularly. You've never used clickers and have no idea how they work. What should you do?

Scenario 6.2 Your TA responsibilities include monitoring an online discussion forum. Some of the students have become increasingly belligerent and intolerant of other students' opinions. What should you do?

Scenario 6.3 In your virtual live-streaming tutorial, several students have their cameras off and are not answering questions or contributing to class discussions. Participation in tutorials counts toward their course mark and you're not sure you'll be able to adequately assess their participation. What should you do?

Possible Scenario Responses

Scenario 6.1 You're a TA in a large lecture section. The instructor has informed you that they'll be using clickers regularly. You've never used clickers and have no idea how they work. What should you do?

↓

Ask the course instructor or another TA how the clickers work. See if you can borrow one to have a closer look and, if possible, ask the instructor to give you a chance to practise in the lecture room. Check the resources for Chapter 6 for more information.

Scenario 6.2 Your TA responsibilities include monitoring an online discussion forum. Some of the students have become increasingly belligerent and intolerant of other students' opinions. What should you do?

↓

Make sure all students are aware of online etiquette and the requirements for appropriate posts. Remind them if necessary. Inform your course supervisor and discuss what further measures could be taken. Inappropriate online behaviour should not be tolerated.

Scenario 6.3 In your virtual live-streaming tutorial, several students have their cameras off and are not answering questions or contributing to class discussions. Participation in tutorials counts toward their course mark and you're not sure you'll be able to adequately assess their participation. What should you do?

↓

Remind students at the beginning of each tutorial that participation counts toward their course mark and that to be adequately assessed they must contribute in class. If students don't have their cameras on, message them privately and ask if there's a problem (there may be extenuating circumstances that are contributing to their lack of video). Set up a way for students to decline to answer when called upon that includes a response on their part, for example, a message in the chat that they wish to pass. That way, you'll know that they are paying attention, and you can call on them again later. Try designing some activities such as filling in a chart or table that require all students to contribute individually.

ASSESSING STUDENT LEARNING

Assessing student learning is an important component of your role as a TA. Most students in higher education are concerned about the marks or grades that they "earn" throughout the course. Not only are marks or grades a component of students' academic self-image, but they're also the key to scholarships and acceptance into specific programs. From the perspective of an instructor or TA, assigning marks or grades is a measure of student learning and provides an opportunity to give feedback and facilitate improvement.

Typically, TAs are not responsible for designing assessments. Course instructors will determine the appropriate forms of assessment, for example, oral presentations, discussion contributions, posters, creative works, written assignments, quizzes, tests, or exams. Students may look to you to help prepare for or complete the work. This is especially true of students who are not familiar with the discipline or its academic standards and may be nervous about interpreting the requirements or the amount of preparation needed.

Office hours and sessions where exam-type questions are reviewed can often help students gain confidence in their abilities. Whatever the format, the assessment should be designed to address specific learning outcomes (see Chapter 3), and the expectations should be transparent to both the TA and the students.

Scenario 7.1 An anxious student has been sending you emails several times a day, including at 2 a.m., prior to a midterm exam. How would you deal with this student and other students with similar concerns?

SUPPORTING STUDENTS WITH ASSESSMENTS

Students are typically keen to know how they're doing in a course. Regular small assignments (quizzes or tests that are graded and contribute a relatively small proportion to course grades) provide students with feedback on their progress in the course and are referred to as formative assessments.

Written comments on students' work can help them improve their performance on similar assignments. Depending on the type of assignment, constructive comments can highlight errors and misconceptions as well as flaws in their writing. But it's also important to provide positive support in the form of comments that indicate work that is well done. In general, comments should be specific and guide the students toward improvement. Start by pointing out what the student has done well and then address some of the areas for improvement, especially those that will be important for subsequent assignments or exams. It's common to have a feedback sandwich near the end of an assignment: list two items done well with one area for improvement in between.

For comments to be useful to students, graded assessments must be returned to the students in a timely fashion, so they can apply the feedback to future assignments and, if necessary, ask for guidance on how to improve their performance on assessments.

EVALUATING STUDENT LEARNING

More heavily weighted assignments such as term papers or final exams are submitted near the end of a course and measure accumulated learning gains. They are a summative evaluation of student learning. Students may not see the marked work, and if that's the case, there's no need for comments to facilitate improvement. If they'll see the marked work, provide comments as you would for formative assessments, including where they received or lost marks.

MARKING GUIDES OR RUBRICS

TAs who mark students' work must be given clear instructions on how the work is to be evaluated. Marking guides or rubrics that indicate mark allocation for different levels of understanding and performance are necessary for consistent and objective assessment. If a rubric or marking guide is not provided, ask the course instructor or supervisor to clarify their expectations for assigning marks or grades. They should be able to discuss with you the expected or necessary content for student answers in an exam or the allocation of marks for content, style, and integration in students' written work. If you're uncertain about whether you're interpreting the instructions correctly or feel that the instructions are insufficient, mark a few assessments and ask your course supervisor about the specific concerns you have. It may also be helpful to discuss the grading with other TAs in the course (current or former).

Scenario 7.2 Your course supervisor has provided you with a detailed and specific rubric for grading an assignment. After marking a few papers, it's apparent to you that some students have reasonable points that are not covered in the rubric. What would you do?

Scenario 7.3 You're not able to complete your marking in the time allotted in your TA hours. You talk to other TAs in the course, and they're not having the same problem. What would you do?

RETURNING MARKED ASSIGNMENTS

Depending on the student's perspective of their abilities and expectations, they may be elated or disheartened when their graded work is returned. Once they become emotional, they won't hear any comments or announcements you might need to make. It's important to relay information about grading-review procedures and the class's overall performance before returning the work.

We recommend that you establish the twenty-four-hour rule: you'll not discuss marks with anyone until at least twenty-four hours have passed. During that time, the students must review the comments (if it's a written assignment) and the mark allocation indicated on the rubric. A good approach is to have them prepare a written list of questions they have about the marking to discuss during a meeting or office hours. If they do this, they'll be better able to discuss the work objectively. In some cases, you may have students who rush up to you after receiving their marked work. Remind them of the twenty-four-hour rule to give them time to calm down.

Occasionally, you may be confronted by an aggressive student. If you suspect this might occur, ask the course supervisor or another TA to be close by. Difficult students should be referred to the supervisor or course instructor. They'll have the authority and experience to respond to the student's questions constructively.

Scenario 7.4 Two students come to you following the return of a midterm exam. They point out that although they have similar answers to a question (similar in thought but different in wording), one was given a higher mark than the other. What could be one source of this discrepancy, and how could it be addressed?

Possible Scenario Responses

Scenario 7.1 An anxious student has been sending you emails several times a day, including at 2 a.m., prior to a midterm exam. How would you deal with this student and others with similar concerns?

↓

Be preemptive. Explain to all students your policy on responding to emails prior to an exam. For example, you may only answer emails until 5 p.m. the day before the exam. Let them know that they should begin preparing for the exam early so that they'll have time to ask their questions before your deadline.

Scenario 7.2 Your course supervisor has provided you with a detailed and specific rubric for grading an assignment. After marking a few papers, it's apparent to you that some students have reasonable points that are not covered in the rubric. What should you do?

↓

Ask your course supervisor if you have any flexibility in interpreting the rubric. Add notes to the rubric as you grade the papers to stay consistent. Discuss the marking with current or former TAs in the course to see if they have any suggestions.

Scenario 7.3 You're not able to complete your marking in the time allotted in your TA hours. You talk to other TAs in the course, and they're not having the same problem. What should you do?

↓

Meet with your course supervisor and see if there are any tips for speeding up your marking.

Scenario 7.4 Two students come to you following the return of a midterm exam. They point out that although they have similar answers to a question (similar in thought but different in wording), one was given a higher mark than the other. What could be one source of this discrepancy, and how could it be addressed?

↓

Although both students felt they provided similar answers, the wording of each student's answer may have communicated different levels of understanding. Use the rubric to indicate where the answers differed.

REFLECTING ON YOUR TEACHING PRACTICE

When you first start to teach, your objective may be to simply time the lesson appropriately, get through the lesson and deliver the material, or lead activities without having trouble answering questions. The planning you do will ensure a successful lesson from your perspective. But will the lesson be effective from the students' perspective? Experienced instructors are aware of how students respond to different elements of the lesson:

◇ Are the students engaged during an activity?

◇ Do they ask relevant questions during the lecture portion of the class?

◇ Are students' responses to polling questions indicating that they're confused about the concepts?

INSIGHT FROM OBSERVATIONS

The behaviour of students during a class is indicative of their level of engagement and can be a valuable form of feedback on your teaching. Collecting information about what's happening in the classroom can be challenging, especially for large classes; however, you may be able to record your lesson and review it later. You might consider asking a peer to observe your lesson and pay particular attention to specific aspects of it. Course supervisors or coordinators may routinely observe your classes, and their feedback can be valuable. Their comments can be the basis for a discussion about your performance and improvements for the future. At most institutions, student evaluations of instructors are mandatory; however, the results are usually not available until after the course is finished. You could ask your students to anonymously provide feedback around the midpoint of the course. This would enable you to act on some of the issues students may have. Be aware that feedback from other sources may not match your perspective. However, it's often extremely valuable.

THINK CAREFULLY ABOUT YOUR TEACHING

As you develop your teaching skills, it's important to review your performance and students' behaviour after each lesson. Self-evaluation on a regular basis is an effective form of professional development. Thinking about your teaching, about why you're creating lessons in a specific format, and objectively considering the effect of the lessons on students will help you to adapt your approach and teaching strategies to meet the needs of the students.

DOCUMENT YOUR REFLECTIONS ON YOUR TEACHING PRACTICE

Observations on your teaching can be collected into a teaching portfolio. Written reflections on innovative activities or teaching situations that did not go as planned can offer valuable insights into your professional development. A selection of these reflections can be included in future applications for teaching positions or promotions.

Scenario 8.1 You've created a lesson that you think is innovative, and you're excited to test a new activity in class. During class, however, you find that the students are either confused by your instructions, don't know what to do, or have given up and have started chatting among themselves. What can you learn from this experience? How could you better understand the difficulties your students were facing with this lesson?

Scenario 8.2 During an instructional skills workshop, you were recorded while giving a lesson to a group of peers. You were extremely anxious during this experience. What could be the value of observing yourself teaching the lesson?

Scenario 8.3 You find that while you're teaching your class, you're unaware of how students in the back half of the classroom are responding to your lesson. What can you do to get the information you need to evaluate your lesson?

PROFESSIONAL DEVELOPMENT

If you pursue a career in academia, you'll likely have a position where you'll be teaching and doing research. To further your professional development and prepare for your future as an educator, it's important to reflect on your teaching experiences, in a journal or as part of a teaching portfolio. List any TA-training workshops, seminars, or discipline-specific education courses that you attend and include a description of the lessons you've learned. Talk to course instructors and designers and ask about their experiences as educators. They may be able to direct you to professional development opportunities at your campus as well as conferences and meetings that may be worthwhile.

LEARNING MORE ABOUT EFFECTIVE TEACHING

Reflecting on your experience in the classroom is personal contemplation of teaching. The next step in your professional development as a TA is to adopt a scholarly approach and learn from publications on pedagogy. The vast educational literature – whether in books, journal articles, or reports – is based on evidence gathered by various methodologies and research protocols. Reading widely will ultimately provide you with valuable insights into teaching practices as well as theories in education, learning, and psychology. The Additional Resources section of this guide provides examples of education literature.

EVIDENCE–BASED TEACHING

The application of teaching strategies from the pedagogical literature, with modifications for your teaching situation, is another step in evidence-based teaching. Once you've tried out these new strategies, how will you know if they're effective and enhance student learning? To answer these questions, you can devise a research project where the basic steps parallel the structure of other discipline-based projects. The first step is to identify a clear goal and specific research question; you can review the pedagogical literature to determine the most appropriate inquiry method. Determine what aspect of your teaching you'll be investigating and the best means of collecting information or data. For example, if you're trying to determine whether a new case-based activity is effective, you could develop a pair of surveys or quizzes that reveal student knowledge before the activity (pre-test) and after the activity (post-test). When you're collecting data, it's important to keep in mind how you'll summarize and analyze the data. The interpretation of the findings of your inquiry project or action research (projects undertaken to directly benefit students) can provide valuable insights into the effectiveness of your teaching practices.

CONTRIBUTING TO THE SCHOLARSHIP OF TEACHING AND LEARNING

The findings of your action research or inquiry project may be of interest to colleagues and other educators in your field. Sharing your contributions through conversations, presentations, posters, and journal articles is a step toward contributing to the scholarship of teaching and learning.

Before your inquiry project can be shared widely in journal articles, you should consider several things. As with any research with human subjects, you must have approval from a board of ethics at your institution. You must guarantee that participants in the inquiry project will not be harmed or disadvantaged. Your research question and findings should be placed in the context of current educational theory and relate to the findings of similar research published in educational journals. Ensure that the methodology you implement is clearly described and designed to provide evidence regarding your research question. You should consider running a small-scale pilot of your study; you may find that the treatment or method of data collection needs to be modified. Once the necessary changes are made, the scaled-up implementation can be carried out with more confidence. If the information or data you collect can be analyzed with statistics, make sure that the statistical methods are rigorous and appropriate for your project. Remember to honour the original intent of the project and to address your research question; often, much interesting information is obtained through these inquiry projects.

Conference presentations are a good means of getting feedback on the interpretation of your data. A formal written description of your research can also be submitted as a journal article, which will undergo review and will provide further feedback. Once published, your article will contribute to the scholarship of teaching and learning (SoTL) literature.

There are a variety of resources and networks to support those interested in pursuing SoTL. Most universities have a teaching and learning centre with experts who lead workshops on action research or teaching-related inquiry projects. Courses for graduate students may be available through the faculty of education or individual departments, and international networks such as the Centre for the Integration of Research, Teaching, and Learning (CIRTL) and BioTAP (US) provide instruction and support in conducting pedagogical research.

Scenario 8.4 You've designed a new worksheet addressing one of the concepts students find difficult and will use it in several tutorials that you teach. What steps would you take to determine whether the worksheet is effective in enhancing student learning of that specific concept?

Scenario 8.5 Your course coordinator learned of your great new worksheet and would like you to share the results of your action research with colleagues. If you were to present your findings to a larger audience as a journal article, what additional steps would you need to take?

Scenario 8.6 After your first experience with education research, you realize that there's more to learn about the scholarship of teaching and learning. What resources could you search for in your institution and internationally?

Possible Scenario Responses

Scenario 8.1 You've created a lesson that you think is innovative, and you're excited to test a new activity in class. During class, however, you find that the students are either confused by your instructions, don't know what to do, or have given up and have started chatting among themselves. What can you learn from this experience? How could you better understand the difficulties your students were facing with this lesson?

↓

Although you may think your activity is clever, ask other TAs or your course instructor if the instructions for the activity are clear and if the challenges are appropriate for the students. During class, if you sense students are having difficulties, ask individual students or survey the class for the main difficulties and provide them with guidance to overcome the problems they're having.

Scenario 8.2 During an instructional skills workshop, you were recorded while giving a lesson to a group of peers. You were extremely anxious during this experience. What could be the value of observing yourself teaching this lesson?

↓

You may notice mannerisms that you were unaware of and may be distracting. You can objectively assess whether your instructions were logical and understandable. You'll likely also notice the strengths of your lesson, which will provide you with the confidence you need to overcome your nervousness when speaking in front of a class.

Scenario 8.3 You find that while you're teaching your class, you're unaware of how students in the back half of the classroom are responding to your lesson. What can you do to get the information you need to evaluate your lesson?

↓

Ask another TA or colleague to peer review your teaching by sitting in the class to observe your teaching. They can report whether students are attentive or if they're disengaged. A trained class observer can use COPUS (https://cwsei.ubc.ca/resources/tools/copus) to record student and instructor activity during the class.

Scenario 8.4 You've designed a new worksheet addressing one of the concepts students find difficult and will use it in several tutorials that you teach. What steps would you take to determine whether the worksheet was effective in enhancing student learning of those specific concepts?

↓

You could compare the learning gains of a group of students that used the worksheet with a group of similar students who did not. If possible, you could use an exam question on the concept to measure their learning and could compare the mean scores from a group in the previous year with the current group or compare students in a class that used the worksheet with another class that did not. Care must be taken to ensure that the groups (or classes) are sufficiently similar (age and gender balance, achievement) to be confident that the worksheet is contributing to any difference in learning gains that you may find.

Scenario 8.5 Your course coordinator learned of your great new worksheet and would like you to share the results of your action research with colleagues. If you were to present your findings to a larger audience as a journal article, what additional steps would you need to take?

↓

If you're sharing your findings with others in formal presentations or journal articles, you must follow Behavioural Research Ethics Board (BREB) protocols. Students will need to give you permission to use their responses. Care must be taken to ensure that your research design is sound and that no group of students has been negatively impacted by the study.

Scenario 8.6 After your first experience with action research, you realize that there's more to learn about the scholarship of teaching and learning. What resources could you search for in your institution and internationally?

⬇

Most universities have teaching and learning centres that hold workshops or have SoTL experts that can provide guidance. Investigate networks on SoTL such as CIRTL (the Centre for the Integration of Research, Teaching, and Learning), BioTAP (the Biology Teaching Assistant Project, US), and ISSOTL (the International Society for the Scholarship of Teaching and Learning).

WORDS OF ENCOURAGEMENT

Developing skills as a teacher takes practice. With experience, you'll collect ideas and skills – such as the suggestions we've provided in this guide – that you can add to your teaching toolbox. With practice, you'll learn to apply the appropriate strategy in each teaching context, whether it's a seminar, tutorial, lecture, field activity, or laboratory experience.

Continue to learn from the experiences of your colleagues, effective instructors, and the teaching and learning centres at your institution. There is much to learn, so take advantage of professional development programs. You're now part of the community of teaching practice, and as you acquire more experience, you too can contribute your perspective during workshops and act as a mentor to TAs who are beginning their exciting and rewarding journey into teaching. Good teachers are lifelong learners.

We hope that the information and advice provided in this guide have enabled you to confidently tackle the challenges of your first teaching experience and will continue to be a useful reference in the future.

ACKNOWLEDGMENTS

The Departments of Botany and Zoology at the University of British Columbia provided a supportive community for teaching and learning initiatives, including TA training. There have been many instructors who have contributed to the Biology Teaching Assistant Program (BioTAP) and graduate students have provided valuable feedback on the information they need to help them transition into their new role as TAs. We thank contributors to the development and facilitation of BioTAP sessions: Ellen Rosenberg, Sunita Chowrira, Pamela Kalas, Angie O'Neill, Robin Young, Chin Sun, Stella Lee, and Christine Goedhart. We also thank graduate students who have served as coordinators for BioTAP and who helped shape a series of successful workshops: Nikta Fay, Adriana Suarez, Evelyn Sun, and Rhea Storlund. Numerous other senior TAs have contributed to the workshops by sharing their experiences with TAs new to the biology program.

In addition, we would like to thank Skylight (the Science Centre for Teaching and Learning) for the many pedagogical programs they offer that have informed and inspired faculty, instructors, and graduate students. We also want to acknowledge the Centre for Teaching, Learning and Technology (CTLT) for the workshops and resources they have developed and delivered over the years. And, finally, we thank the vice-provost and associate vice-president academic affairs for their financial support of BioTAP and the continuing support from the Botany and Zoology Departments at UBC.

APPENDIX: DEVELOPING TRAINING OPPORTUNITIES FOR TAS

Teaching assistants with experience and insights into teaching are often asked to help with TA-training workshops and are looked upon as role models for new TAs. Novice TAs often feel the need for instruction on teaching but may be unaware of opportunities that exist on campus or through online programs. If you're a course supervisor or experienced TA, you can help new TAs by suggesting training opportunities that may already be in place at your institution. For example, look for instructional skills workshops (ISWs), programs from your teaching and learning centre, and the Centre for the Integration of Research, Teaching, and Learning (CIRTL). These programs address universal best practices that can be applied to teaching in different disciplines and roles. If your program or academic unit does not have TA-training workshops, and you have an interest in delving into TA training, consider developing a workshop on an aspect of teaching that is most needed in your discipline.

WHAT TO CONSIDER IN DESIGNING A WORKSHOP

If you decide to design your own workshops, there are several things to keep in mind. TAs are usually a diverse group with different cultural backgrounds, undergraduate experiences, levels of confidence, and linguistic competence. How will you provide basic training for pedagogical novices with diverse backgrounds and at the same time have something to offer more experienced TAs? Can you enlist the support of senior TAs to help develop activities and support for new TAs?

In addition, as discussed in Chapter 1, TAs may have different roles in instructional support, for example, they may teach tutorials, seminars, or labs, assist in lectures, have an online role, or may be primarily responsible for marking. Some TAs may not know the content or learning outcomes of what they'll be teaching; others may be involved in developing some of the content and assessments. Will you have different sessions for specific roles? TAs may be assigned the same or different courses each term, so new skills should be transferable.

Often, TAs have a variety of time commitments; they may be doing research, working on art or music projects, caring for family members, and so on, which may make scheduling meetings or workshops difficult. Will you have sessions online, or during daytime, evening, or weekend hours?

The motivation of TAs is also important to consider. If they are TAs simply for financial support, they may not be willing to invest time and effort into professional development. Will your TA training be required or voluntary? If the training is mandatory and part of their TA duties, they may need to be paid for their time.

Finally, consider the scope of your workshops. Will your TA training be targeted to TAs in your department or offered to all TAs in your faculty or institution?

TOPICS TO ADDRESS

The topics you address in your workshops should be determined by the needs of the participants. It's important to survey new TAs to determine which aspects of teaching they want to explore. Many of the essential topics in this guide could be considered as potential foci of your training sessions. You might want to include the following topics:

◇ planning and preparing to teach

◇ ways to create a safe, supportive, and inclusive student-learning environment

◇ how to enhance student engagement and develop a sense of community and ownership

◇ effective classroom management and general teaching practices

◇ teaching strategies and modes of instruction, including active learning techniques

◇ effective use of in-class facilities (e.g., computers, whiteboards, doc cams, clickers)

◇ assessment of student learning and the alignment of learning outcomes with activities.

Many resources provide guidance and useful materials for TA-training programs. An entire section of Jo Handelsman, Sarah Miller, and Christine Pfund's *Scientific Teaching* (2007) is devoted to planning guides for a variety of workshops on topics such as scientific (evidence-based) teaching, active learning, assessment, and diversity. This resource and others may provide helpful ideas for your sessions.

THE FORM OF TA TRAINING

TA training can take many different forms, ranging from individual mentoring to formal courses or even international programs. The form of TA training you develop will depend on the needs of the TAs in your program and the TA training already available in your institution. An easy way to get started is to initiate informal mentoring programs where experienced TAs or instructors guide new TAs through the teaching experience. Regular weekly or monthly sessions such as "brown bag lunches" that focus on general pedagogical topics can include guest speakers, journal article discussions, and reports on scholarship of teaching and learning (SoTL) projects. These are easy to organize and foster a sense of a teaching community.

More formally, there can be course-level TA preparation, which usually consists of weekly sessions to prepare for the coming lessons. There can also be department- or program-based sessions that might include a beginning-of-term orientation for new TAs. These can be one- to three-day sessions that introduce TAs to institutional policies and prepare them to teach their first classes. Some departments or faculties may be agreeable to offering credit courses, which allow in-depth study of a variety of pedagogical topics and could include discussions, guest speakers, classroom observations, development of mini-lessons, and research projects. Courses that add one to three credits to graduate student programs need to be approved by administrators. If timing and logistics are a barrier, it's also possible to produce virtual orientation packages consisting of videos on a range of topics. These can be made available online for TAs to view as needed.

This approach, however, reduces the sense of community that is fostered when sessions are held in person.

Modelling of best practices in teaching in the implementation of your TA-training sessions is important. This includes elements of reflective practice. Be sure to ask participants to evaluate your workshops either through surveys or focus groups or by requesting anonymous comments. The comments you receive can guide you in making changes to future iterations of your TA-training program.

Developing all but the most basic TA-training sessions will require funding, the cooperation of your department, and considerable effort. It will not be easy, but in the absence of other programs, it will be an important and rewarding experience for the designer and participants.

ADDITIONAL RESOURCES

GETTING STARTED

Hoessler, C., and L. Godden. 2015. "The Visioning of Policy and the Hope of Implementation: Support for Graduate Students' Teaching at a Canadian Institution." *Canadian Journal of Higher Education* 45, 1: 83–101.

Parker, M.A., D. Ashe, J. Boersma, R. Hicks, and V. Bennett. 2015. "Good Teaching Starts Here: Applied Learning at the Graduate Teaching Assistant Institute." *Canadian Journal of Higher Education* 45: 84–110. **An excellent review of the literature to 2015.**

CHAPTER 1: STEPPING INTO YOUR ROLE

Arbach, M. 2011. "Being Professional in Your Teaching Assistant Position." *Ethical Issues for Teaching Assistants*. Centre for University Teaching, University of Ottawa. https://tlss.uottawa.ca/site/images/1-TLSS/TA/documents/TAv1n5_EN.pdf.

BioTap, University of British Columbia. n.d. "Expectations." https://blogs.ubc.ca/biotap/getting-ready-to-teach/.

Dalhousie University. n.d. *Instructor/Student Relationships: A Guide for Faculty and Teaching Assistants*. https://cdn.dal.ca/content/dam/dalhousie/pdf/dept/hres/brochures/Instructor-Student%20Relationships.pdf.

Gwenna Moss Centre for Teaching and Learning, University of Saskatchewan. 2017. *Expectations of TAs*. https://teaching.usask.ca/articles/graduate-teacher-expectations.php.

Isabeau Iqbal, ed. 2005–6. *University Teaching and Learning: An Instructional Resource Guide for Teaching Assistants*. Vancouver: Centre for Teaching and Academic Growth, UBC.

Teaching Assistants' Training Program, University of Toronto. n.d. "Your Relationship with the Course Instructor." https://tatp.utoronto.ca/teaching-toolkit/first-time-taing/relationship-course-instructor/.

CHAPTER 2: PREPARING FOR YOUR FIRST SESSION

Chickering, A.W., and Z.F. Gamson. 1987. "Seven Principles for Good Practice in Undergraduate Education." *AAHE Bulletin* (March): https://aahea.org/articles/sevenprinciples1987.htm.

Persky, A.M. 2012. *Educational Blueprints*. Chapel Hill, NC: LLC.

CHAPTER 3: DESIGNING LESSONS AND LEARNING ACTIVITIES

Allen, D., and K.D. Tanner. 2009. "Talking to Learn: Why Undergraduate Biology Students Should Be Talking in Classrooms." In *Transformations: Approaches to College Science Teaching*, 26–39. New York: W.H. Freeman and Company. **This publication is an excellent resource for many topics.**

–. 2009. "Questions about Questions." In *Transformations*, 40–50. **This chapter has excellent information on Bloom's taxonomy.**

Bloom, B.S., M.D. Englehart, E.J. Furst, W.H. Hill, and D.R. Krathwohl. 1956. *A Taxonomy of Educational Objectives Handbook. Book I, Cognitive Domain*. New York: McKay.

Centre for Community Engaged Learning, University of British Columbia. n.d. "Action Words for Bloom's Taxonomy." https://students.ubc.ca/sites/students.ubc.ca/files/Bloom%27s%20Taxonomy%20Verbs%20list.pdf.

Freeman, S., S.L. Eddy, M. McDonough, M.K. Smith, N. Okoroafor, H. Jordt, and M.P. Wenderoth. 2014. "Active Learning Increases Student Performance in Science, Engineering, and Mathematics." *PNAS* 11, 23: 8410–15.

Handelsman, J., S. Miller, and C. Pfund. 2007. "Active Learning." In *Scientific Teaching*, 23–45. New York: W.H. Freeman and Company.

CHAPTER 4: CREATING AN INCLUSIVE LEARNING ENVIRONMENT

Allen, D., and K.D. Tanner. 2009. "Cultural Competence in the College Biology Classroom." In *Transformations: Approaches to College Science Teaching*, 167–83. New York: W.H. Freeman and Company.

–. 2009. "Learning Styles and the Problem of Instructional Selection: Engaging All Students in Science Courses." In *Transformations*, 143–54.

CBE-Life Sciences Education. n.d. "Evidence-Based Teaching Guides: Inclusive Teaching." https://lse. ascb.org/evidence-based-teaching-guides/ inclusive-teaching/?_ ga=2.183723493.2145196098.1621802003– 1090182875.1620759684. **This is an excellent, easy-to-use guide, with examples. Although geared to teaching in STEM, many of the suggestions are transferable to all disciplines. It includes a section on developing self-awareness, which may be useful in uncovering your own social and professional identity.**

Centre for Teaching, Learning and Technology, University of British Columbia. 2019. "Inclusive Course Design." https://ctlt-inclusiveteaching.

sites.olt.ubc.ca/files/2019/01/Inclusive-Course
-Design_w.pdf.

Cooper, K.M., A.J.J. Auerbach, J.D. Bader, A.S. Bea-
dles-Bohling, J.A. Brashears, E. Cline, S.L. Eddy,
D.B. Elliott, E. Farley, L. Fuselier, et al. 2020.
"Fourteen Recommendations to Create a More
Inclusive Environment for LGBTQ+ Individuals in
Academic Biology." *CBE-Life Sciences Education*
19, 3: https://doi.org/10.1187/cbe.20–04–0062.

Dewsbury, B., and C.J. Brame. 2019. "Inclusive Teaching." *CBE-Life Sciences Education* 18, 2: https://doi.
org/10.1187/cbe.19–01–0021.

Hales, K.G. 2020. "Signaling Inclusivity in Undergraduate Biology Courses through Deliberate Framing
of Genetics Topics Relevant to Gender Identity,
Disability, and Race." *CBE-Life Sciences Education*
19, 2: https://doi.org/10.1187/cbe.19–08–0156.

Handelsman, J., S. Miller, and C. Pfund. 2007. "Diversity." In *Scientific Teaching,* 65–82. New York: W.H.
Freeman and Company.

Kendi, I.X. 2019. *How to Be an Antiracist.* New York:
One World.

Kimmerer, R.W. 2013. *Braiding Sweetgrass: Indigenous
Wisdom, Scientific Knowledge, and the Teachings of
Plants*. Minneapolis, MN: Milkweed.

King, T. 2013. *The Inconvenient Indian: A Curious
Account of Native People in North America.*
Toronto: Penguin Random House.

Pfeifer, M.A., E.M. Reiter, J.J. Cordero, and J.D.
Stanton. 2021. "Inside and Out: Factors That
Support and Hinder the Self-Advocacy of Under-
graduates with ADHD and/or Specific Learning
Disabilities in STEM." *CBE-Life Sciences Education*
20, 2: https://doi.org/10.1187/cbe.20–06–0107.

Tanner, K., and D. Allen. 2017. "Cultural Competence
in the College Biology Classroom." *CBE-Life Sciences Education* 6, 4: https://doi.org/10.1187/
cbe.07–09–0086.

Tanner, K.D. 2013. "Structure Matters: Twenty-One
Teaching Strategies to Promote Student Engagement and Cultivate Classroom Equity." *CBE-Life
Sciences Education* 12, 3: https://doi.org/10.1187/
cbe.13-06-0115.

UBC. 2014. "UBC Statement on Respectful Environment for Students, Faculty and Staff." https://
hr.ubc.ca/sites/default/files/wp-content/blogs.
dir/14/files/UBC-Statement-on-Respectful
-Environment-2014.pdf.

CHAPTER 5: FACILITATING CLASSROOM INTERACTION

Allen, D., and K.D. Tanner. 2009. "Answers Worth
Waiting For: One Second Is Hardly Enough." In
*Transformations: Approaches to College Science
Teaching,* 19–25. New York: W.H. Freeman and
Company.

–. 2009. "Cooperative Learning: Beyond Working in Groups." In *Transformations,* 155–66.

–. 2009. "Questions about Questions." In *Transformations,* 40–50.

Bain, K. 2004. "How Do They Conduct Class?" In *What the Best College Teachers Do,* 98–134. Cambridge, MA: Harvard University Press.

Center for Excellence in Teaching and Learning, University of Connecticut. "Leading Effective Discussions." n.d. https://cetl.uconn.edu/resources/teaching-your-course/leading-effective-discussions/.

Centre for Teaching Excellence, University of Waterloo. "Facilitating Effective Discussions." https://uwaterloo.ca/centre-for-teaching-excellence/teaching-resources/teaching-tips/alternatives-lecturing/discussions/facilitating-effective-discussions.

Harper, S.R., and C.H.F. Davis III. 2016. "Eight Actions to Reduce Racism in College Classrooms." https://www.aaup.org/article/eight-actions-reduce-racism-college-classrooms#.YUjXpbhKiUl.

Harriet W. Sheridan Center for Teaching and Learning, Brown University. n.d. "Tips on Facilitating Effective Group Discussions." https://www.brown.edu/sheridan/teaching-learning-resources/teaching-resources/classroom-practices/learning-contexts/discussions/tips.

Mejia, S. 2021. Chicago Center for Teaching and Learning. "Leading Effective Discussion." https://teaching.uchicago.edu/resources/foundations-of-teaching-learning/leading-discussion-sections/.

Oakley, B., R.M. Felder, R. Brent, and I.H. Elhajj. 2004. "Turning Student Groups into Effective Teams." *Journal of Student Centred Learning* 2 1: 9–34.

Pfund, C., J. Branchaw, and J. Handelsman. 2014. *Entering Mentoring*. New York: W.H. Freeman and Company.

Wilson, K.J., P. Brickman, and C.J. Brame. 2018. "Group Work." *CBE-Life Sciences Education* 17, 1: https://doi.org/10.1187/cbe.17–12–0258.

CHAPTER 6: TEACHING WITH TECHNOLOGY

Arts ISIT Instructional Resources and Information Technology, University of British Columbia. n.d. *Ideas and Strategies for Using Classroom Response Systems*. https://isit.arts.ubc.ca/classroom-response-systems-strategy/. **(Includes a list of additional resources.)**

Centre for Teaching, Learning and Technology, University of British Columbia. n.d. *List of Learning Technologies*. https://ctlt.ubc.ca/learning-technologies/.

Prud'homme-Généreux, A. 2021. "21 Ways to Structure an Online Discussion." *Higher Ed Teaching Strategies from Magna Publications.* This is a five-part online series, starting here: https://www.facultyfocus.com/articles/online-education/online-student-engagement/21-ways-to-structure-an-online-discussion-part-1/.

CHAPTER 7: ASSESSING STUDENT LEARNING

Allen, D., and K.D. Tanner. 2009. "How Can I Know That My Students Are Learning?" In *Transformations: Approaches to College Science Teaching,* 69–110. New York: W.H. Freeman and Company.

Alters, B, and S. Alters. 2005. "Assessment." In *Teaching Biology in Higher Education,* 51–70. Hoboken, NJ: John Wiley and Sons.

Bain, K. 2004. "How Do They Evaluate Their Students and Themselves?" In *What the Best College Teachers Do,* 150–72. Cambridge, MA: Harvard University Press.

Dirks, C., M.P. Wenderoth, and M. Withers. 2014. "Assessment in Practice." In *Assessment in the College Classroom,* 41–104. New York: W.H. Freeman and Company.

Handelsman, J., S. Miller, and C. Pfund. 2007. "Assessment." In *Scientific Teaching,* 47–64. New York: W.H. Freeman and Company.

CHAPTER 8: REFLECTING ON YOUR TEACHING PRACTICE

Allen, D., and K.D. Tanner. 2009. "How Can I Continue My Professional Growth in Science Education?" In *Transformations: Approaches to College Science Teaching,* 213–24. New York: W.H. Freeman and Company.

Alters, B., and S. Alters, S. 2005. "Educational Research and Improving Teaching." In *Teaching Biology in Higher Education,* 1–17. Hoboken, NJ: John Wiley and Sons.

British Council/BBC. 2004. "Reflective Teaching: Exploring Our Own Classroom Practice." https://www.teachingenglish.org.uk/article/reflective-teaching-exploring-our-own-classroom-practice.

Centre for the Integration of Research, Teaching, and Learning (CIRTL), University of British Columbia. n.d. "About." http://cirtl.ubc.ca/.

CIRTL Network, Center for the Integration of Research, Teaching, and Learning. "Upcoming Events." https://www.cirtl.net/.

Finlay, L. 2008. "Reflecting on 'Reflective' Practice." Paper prepared for the Practice-Based Professional Learning Centre, the Open University. http://ncsce.net/wp-content/uploads/2016/10/Finlay-2008-Reflecting-on-reflective-practice-PBPL-paper-52.pdf.

Handelsman, J., S. Miller, and C. Pfund. 2007. "Scientific Teaching." In *Scientific Teaching,* 1–18. New

York: W.H. Freeman and Company.

Hutchings, P., and L.E. Shulman. 1999. "The Scholarship of Teaching: New Elaborations, New Developments." *Change* 31, 5: https://doi.org/10.1080/00091389909604218.

International Society for the Scholarship of Teaching and Learning (ISSOTL). n.d. "About." https://issotl.com/.

McKinney, K. 2006. "Attitudinal and Structural Factors Contributing to Challenges in the Work of the Scholarship of Teaching and Learning." *New Directions for Institutional Research* 129 (Summer): https://doi.org/10.1002/ir.170.

Smith. M.K., F.H.M. Jones, S.L. Gilbert, and C.E. Wieman. 2013. "The Classroom Observation Protocol for Undergraduate STEM (COPUS): A New Instrument to Characterize University STEM Classroom Practices." *CBE-Life Sciences Education* 12, 4: https://www.lifescied.org/doi/10.1187/cbe.13-08-0154.

University of Tennessee Knoxville. n.d. "Biology Teaching Assistant Project (BioTAP)." https://biotap.org/.

WORDS OF ENCOURAGEMENT

Centre for Teaching, Learning and Technology, University of British Columbia. 2018. "CTLT programs/CoP Overview." https://wiki.ubc.ca/Documentation:CTLT_programs/CoP_Overview.

Mercieca, B. 2017. "What Is a Community of Practice?" In *Communities of Practice: Facilitating Social Learning in Higher Education,* edited by J. McDonald and A. Cater-Steel, 3–25. Singapore: Springer.

–. 2018. "Communities of Practice: Want to Keep Early Career Teachers in the Job? Do This." *Edu Research Matters*, November 27. https://www.aare.edu.au/blog/?tag=communities-of-practice.

APPENDIX

Centre for Teaching and Learning, Western University. "Teaching Assistant Training Program (TATP)." n.d. https://teaching.uwo.ca/programs/allprograms/tatp.html.

Centre for Teaching Support and Innovation, University of Toronto. n.d. https://teaching.utoronto.ca.

Handelsman, J., S. Miller, and C. Pfund. 2007. "Scientific Teaching Workshops." In *Scientific Teaching,* 123–63. New York: W.H. Freeman and Company.

McGill University, AGSEM Teaching Assistant Training. n.d. "Workshops and Resources." https://www.mcgill.ca/skillsets/offerings/teaching-assistant-training.

ABOUT THE AUTHORS

Kathy Nomme has forty years of teaching experience, first teaching biology at a high school and then in the Departments of Botany and Zoology at the University of British Columbia (UBC). She trained as a high school teacher at Simon Fraser University in the Professional Development Program. At UBC, she has participated in and led many teaching-related workshops. In 2009, she completed the Faculty Certificate Program on Teaching and Learning in Higher Education and has been a co-instructor of BIOL 535, Teaching and Learning in the Life Sciences. As a biology instructor and coordinator of a large enrolment laboratory course, she developed effective means of preparing graduate student TAs for their important role in undergraduate courses. In 2012, she joined the group of instructors offering a TA orientation. In subsequent years, she was instrumental in developing TA-training efforts into a series of seven workshops, now known as BioTAP. She has undertaken several pedagogical research projects and collaborated with the Centre for Teaching, Learning and Technology and Skylight (the Science Centre for Teaching and Learning) at UBC with regard to promoting effective teaching practices and enhancing student learning. She is a professor of teaching emerita and continues to be involved in projects related to improving the learning experience for undergraduate students.

Carol Pollock is a professor of teaching emerita in the Department of Zoology at the University of British Columbia. She was first hired as a sessional lecturer at UBC in 1980 and from that time until her retirement at the end of 2016 she was involved with preparing TAs for their roles in the labs and lectures in the courses she taught. In the 1990s, she expanded this to include professional development for all TAs in biology undergraduate courses (now called BioTAP). BioTAP has evolved from a single session at the beginning of September to seven sessions throughout the academic year. In 2014, she was asked to be part of a committee to establish national standards for TA training in the United States (also called BioTAP), and she continues to work with this committee. In addition to TA training, some of her other areas of interest and research have been the pedagogy of investigative learning, self-regulated learning, scientific teaching, concept inventories, and peer teaching.